UNSTOPPABLE

ALSO BY NICK VUJICIC

Life Without Limits

NICK VUJICIC

UNSTOPPABLE

The Incredible Power *of* Faith *in* Action

WATERBROOK
PRESS

UNSTOPPABLE
PUBLISHED BY WATERBROOK PRESS
12265 Oracle Boulevard, Suite 200
Colorado Springs, Colorado 80921

This book is not intended to replace or substitute the diagnosis, evaluation, or advice of a health-care professional. Readers are advised to consult a physician, therapist, or other qualified health-care professional regarding diagnosis or treatment of their health problems. The author and publisher specifically disclaim liability, loss, or risk, personal or otherwise, which is incurred as a consequence, directly or indirectly, of the use or application of any of the contents of this book.

Scripture quotations are taken or paraphrased from the following versions: King James Version. The Holy Bible, New International Version®, NIV®. Copyright © 1973, 1978, 1984 by Biblica Inc.™ Used by permission of Zondervan. All rights reserved worldwide. www.zondervan.com. The New King James Version®. Copyright © 1982 by Thomas Nelson Inc. Used by permission. All rights reserved. The Holy Bible, New Living Translation, copyright © 1996, 2004, 2007. Used by permission of Tyndale House Publishers Inc., Carol Stream, Illinois 60188. All rights reserved.

Italics in Scripture quotations reflect the author's added emphasis.

Details in some anecdotes and stories have been changed to protect the identities of the persons involved.

ISBN 978-0-307-73153-1
ISBN 978-0-307-73090-9 (electronic)

Cover design by Kristopher K. Orr; cover photography by Allen Mozo

Published in the United States by WaterBrook Multnomah, an imprint of the Crown Publishing Group, a division of Random House Inc., New York.

WATERBROOK and its deer colophon are registered trademarks of Random House Inc.

Library of Congress Cataloging-in-Publication Data
Vujicic, Nick.
   Unstoppable : the incredible power of faith in action / Nick Vujicic. — 1st ed.
     p. cm.
   ISBN 978-0-307-73088-6 — ISBN 978-0-307-73090-9 (electronic)
  1. Faith. 2. Encouragement—Religious aspects—Christianity 3. Inspiration—Religious aspects—Christianity. 4. Success—Religious aspects—Christianity. I. Title.
   BV4637.V625 2012
   248.8'6—dc23
                                                    2012013071

Printed in the United States of America
2012—First International Trade Paperback Edition

10 9 8 7 6

SPECIAL SALES
Most WaterBrook Multnomah books are available at special quantity discounts when purchased in bulk by corporations, organizations, and special-interest groups. Custom imprinting or excerpting can also be done to fit special needs. For information, please e-mail SpecialMarkets@WaterBrookMultnomah.com or call 1-800-603-7051.

In loving memory of the father-in-law I'll meet in heaven,
Kiyoshi Miyahara.

I dedicate this book to my wife,
Kanae Loida Vujicic-Miyahara,
my greatest gift and joy ever, after salvation itself.

CONTENTS

Introduction

WELCOME TO MY SECOND BOOK. MY NAME IS NICK VUJICIC (PRONOUNCED *Voo-yi-chich*). Even if you did not read my first book, *Life Without Limits,* you may have seen my videos on YouTube or attended one of my appearances around the world as an inspirational speaker and evangelist.

As you probably know or can see from my cover photograph, I was born without arms or legs. What you cannot see but might have sensed already is that my lack of limbs has not kept me from enjoying great adventures, a fulfilling and meaningful career, and loving relationships. In this book my goal is to share with you the unstoppable power of faith in action that has helped me create my own ridiculously good life, despite my disabilities.

Putting faith in action is about believing and achieving. It's about having faith in yourself, your talents, your purpose, and, most of all, in God's love and His divine plan for your life.

This book was inspired by the many people of all ages from around the world who've asked me for advice and guidance in dealing with specific challenges in their own lives. They know from my speeches that I have overcome adversities, including my youthful thoughts of suicide, concerns about being able to support myself and whether I'd ever find a woman to love me, my experiences with bullying, and other issues and insecurities that are not unique to me by any means.

The chapter topics address the most common questions and challenges people raise when they speak and write to me, including

- personal crises
- relationship issues
- career and job challenges
- health and disability concerns
- self-destructive thoughts, emotions, and addictions
- bullying, persecution, cruelty, and intolerance
- dealing with matters beyond our control
- how to reach out and serve others
- finding balance in body, mind, heart, and spirit

I hope that sharing my stories and those of others who have persevered through their own trials and hardships—many of them far greater than mine—will help and inspire you to overcome whatever challenges you face. I don't have all the answers, of course. But I have benefitted from wonderful advice from many wise people as well as the love and blessings of my heavenly Father.

I think you will find the guidance in these pages practical as well as inspiring. It's important to keep in mind as you read that you are never alone. Help is available from friends, family members, teachers, counselors, and clergy. Don't think you have to handle your burdens by yourself.

Remember, too, that there are probably many others who've faced and met the same challenges you encounter. This book also will share the stories of people I know and stories from others who have written to me to share their experiences. In some cases I've changed their names, but the stories are authentic and always inspiring for the courage, faith, and perseverance they exhibit.

As a boy trying to come to terms with my disabilities, I made the mistake of thinking no one else hurt like I did and that my problems were insurmountable. I thought that my lack of limbs was proof that God did not love me and that my life had no purpose. I also felt that I could not share my burdens—even with those who loved and cared about me.

I was wrong on all counts. I was not alone in my suffering. In fact, many people have dealt with challenges that surpass mine. And God not only loves me, He created me for purposes that I never could have envisioned as a child. He uses me in ways that continue to surprise and amaze me each and every day.

Know that as long as you are on this earth, there is a purpose and a plan for you too. God loves you, and there are many people around you—loved ones and professionals—willing to help you with your challenges. The burdens you carry may seem daunting, but as you will see in the pages that follow, the power of faith in action is truly incredible.

To begin to understand this, simply keep in mind that this man with no arms and no legs travels the world, reaching out to millions of people, while blessed with joy and love beyond measure. I am as imperfect as anyone you will ever meet. I have good days and bad. Challenges rise up and knock me flat on occasion. Yet I know that where I am weak, God is strong, and when we put faith into action, we are unstoppable.

ONE

Faith in Action

Near the end of my 2011 speaking tour in Mexico, an official with the US embassy in Mexico City called to inform me that my US work visa had been put on hold for "a national security investigation."

I live in the United States on that visa because I am a native of Australia. I could not return to my California home without it. Since my staff had scheduled an upcoming series of speaking engagements in the United States, this was a serious problem.

I scrambled to the US embassy with Richie, my caregiver, early the next morning to try to figure out how my visa had anything to do with national security. When we arrived, we found the large reception area packed with people dealing with their own issues. We had to take a number, like in a bakery. The wait was so long I had a nice nap before we finally were called to meet with an official.

When I'm nervous, I turn to humor. It doesn't always work. "Is there a problem with my fingerprints on the visa?" I joked. The embassy person glared at me. Then he called his supervisor. (Maybe my sense of humor was posing a threat to American security?)

The supervisor arrived, also looking quite grim. Visions of being behind bars crept into my head.

"Your name has been tagged as part of an investigation," the supervisor stated robotically. "You can't return to the United States until this is cleared up, and that will take up to a month."

The blood drained from my body. *This cannot be happening!*

Richie collapsed to the ground. At first I thought he'd fainted, but he had dropped to his knees in prayer in front of two hundred people. Yes, he's a very caring caregiver. He raised his arms and his hands together, asking God for a miracle to get us home.

Everything around me seemed to be in fast-forward and slow motion at the same time. As my head whirled, the embassy official added that my name probably was flagged because I travel so much around the world.

Did they suspect me of being an international terrorist? an arms dealer with no arms? Honest, I hadn't laid a hand on anyone. (See what happens when I'm nervous? Make me stop!)

"Come on, seriously, how dangerous could I be?" I asked the embassy official. "I'm meeting with Mexico's president and his wife at the presidential house tomorrow for a Three Kings Day party, so obviously *they* don't see me as a threat."

The US official was not moved. "I don't care if you're meeting with President Obama, you aren't reentering the United States until this investigation is completed," he said.

The situation might have been funny if my schedule hadn't been packed with a long list of speaking engagements back in the good old US of A. I had to get home.

I was not about to sit around and wait for someone to decide that Americans were safe with Nick in the house. I pleaded with the embassy official for several more minutes, explaining my obligations, dropping the names of important people, stressing that I had employees who counted on me and orphans who looked up to me.

He checked with someone higher in rank on the phone. "All they can do is try to expedite the process. It will still take at least two weeks," he said.

I probably had a dozen appearances scheduled for those two weeks. But the embassy official was not sympathetic. All we could do at that point was return to our hotel, where I frantically began calling everyone I knew for help and prayers.

I was tapping into the power of faith in action.

To simply say "I believe" in something is not enough. If you want to have an impact in this world, you must put your beliefs and your faith into action. In this case I tapped into my belief in the power of prayer. I called our team at my nonprofit organization, Life Without Limbs (LWL), in California and asked them to start a prayer chain. "We're moving up the chain of command—way up!" I told them.

The staff at LWL made a flurry of phone calls and sent out a flood of e-mails, tweets, and text messages. Within an hour, one hundred fifty people were praying for a quick resolution to my visa challenge. I also put out calls to friends and supporters who might have influence, relatives, neighbors, or former classmates in the US State Department.

Three hours later, someone from the embassy in Mexico called me. "I can't believe this, but you've been cleared," the official said. "The investigation is over. You can come pick up your renewed US visa tomorrow morning."

That, my friend, is the power of faith in action! It can move mountains, and it can move Nick out of Mexico too.

ACTING IN FAITH

In my travels around the world, people faced with challenges ask me for my advice and my prayers. Often, they know what they need to do, but they are afraid to make a change or to take the first step by asking for help or trusting in God. You, too, may be facing challenges that have you feeling helpless, scared, stuck, paralyzed, uncertain, and unable to act. I understand. I've been there. When teens and young adults come to me and tell me they are being bullied, that they feel lost and alone in the world, or that they are scared because of disabilities, illness, or self-destructive thoughts, I know exactly where they are coming from.

My physical challenges are easy to see, yet people only have to talk to me or hear me speak for a few minutes to understand how much joy I have in spite of that. So they often ask me how I stay positive and where I find the strength to overcome my disabilities. My answer, always, is, "I pray for God's help, and then I put my faith in action." I have faith. I believe in certain things that I have no tangible proof of—things I cannot see, taste, touch, smell, or hear. Most of all, I have faith in God. Though I can't see or touch Him, I believe He created me for a purpose, and I believe that when I put my faith and my beliefs into action, I put myself in a position for God's blessings.

Will I always get what *I* want? No! But I will always get what *God* wants. The same is true for you. Whether you are a Christian or not, you must never think that simply believing in something is enough. You can believe in your dreams, but you have to take action to make them happen. You can believe in your talents and have faith in your abilities, but if you don't develop them and put them to use, what good are they? You can believe that you are a good and caring person, but if you don't treat others with goodness and care, where is the proof?

You have a choice. You can believe or not believe. But *if* you believe— *whatever* you believe—you must act upon it. Otherwise, why believe? You may have had challenges in your career, your relationships, or your health. Maybe you have been mistreated, abused, or discriminated against. All those things that have happened *to* you do define you or your life *if* you fail to take action to define yourself. You can believe in your talents. You can believe that you have love to give. You can believe that you can overcome your illness or disability. But that belief on its own won't bring positive change in your life.

You must put it into action.

If you believe you can change your life for the better or make a positive mark in your town or your state or your world, act upon those beliefs. If you think you have a great idea for starting your own business, you must invest your time, money, and talents and make that business happen. Otherwise, what good is just having the idea? If you have identified someone whom you'd like to spend the rest of your life with, why not act upon that belief? What have you got to lose?

FAITH IN ACTION REWARDED

Having faith, beliefs, and convictions is a great thing, but your life is measured by the actions you take based upon them. You can build a great life around those things you believe and have faith in. I've built mine around my belief that I can inspire and bring hope to people facing challenges in their lives. That belief is rooted in my faith in God. I have faith that He put me on this earth to love, inspire, and encourage others and especially to help all who are willing to accept Jesus Christ as their Lord and Savior. I believe that I can never earn my way to heaven, and by faith I accept the gift of the forgiveness of sins through Christ Jesus. However, there's so much more than just "getting in" through the Pearly Gates. It is also about seeing others changed by the power of His Holy Spirit, having a close relationship with Jesus Christ throughout this life, and then being further rewarded in heaven.

Being born without arms and legs was not God's way of punishing me. I know that now. I have come to realize that this "disability" would actually heighten my ability to serve His purpose as a speaker and evangelist. You might be tempted to think that I'm making a huge leap of faith to feel that way, since most people consider my lack of limbs a huge handicap. Instead, God has used my lack of limbs to draw people to me, especially others with disabilities, so I can inspire and encourage them with my messages of faith, hope, and love.

In the Bible, James said that our actions, not our words, are the proof of our faith. He wrote in James 2:18, "Now someone may argue, 'Some people have faith; others have good deeds.' But I say, 'How can you show me your faith if you don't have good deeds? I will show you my faith by my good deeds.'"

I've heard it said that our *actions* are to our faith and beliefs as our *bodies* are to our spirits. Your body is the housing of your spirit, the evidence of its existence. In the same way, your actions are the evidence of your faith and beliefs. You have no doubt heard the term "walking the talk." Your family, friends, teachers, bosses, coworkers, customers, and clients all expect you to act and live in alignment with the beliefs and convictions that you claim to have. If you don't, they will call you out, won't they?

Our peers judge us not by what we say but by what we do. If you claim to be a good wife and mother, then you sometimes will have to put your family's interests above your own. If you believe your purpose is to share your artistic talents with the world, then you will be judged on the works you produce, not on those you merely propose. You have to walk the talk; otherwise you have no credibility with others—or with yourself—because you, too, should demand that your actions match your words. If they don't, you will never live in harmony and fulfillment.

As a Christian, I believe the final judge of how we've lived is God. The Bible teaches that His judgment is based on our actions, not our words. Revelation 20:12 says, "And I saw the dead, small and great, stand before God; and the books were opened: and another book was opened, which is the book of life: and the dead were judged out of those things which were written in the books, *according to their works*." I act upon my beliefs by traveling the world and encouraging people to love one another and to love God. I am fulfilled in that purpose. I truly believe it is why I was created. When you act upon your beliefs and put your faith into action, you, too, will experience fulfillment. And please, do not be discouraged if you aren't always absolutely confident in your purpose and how to act upon it. I have struggled. I still struggle. And so will you. I fail and am far from perfect. But deeds are merely the fruit—the result of the depth of a true conviction of the truth. Truth is what sets us free, not purpose. I found my purpose because I was looking for truth.

It is hard to find purpose or good in difficult circumstances, but that is the journey. Why did it have to be a journey? Why couldn't a helicopter just pick you up and carry you to the finish line? Because throughout the difficult times, you will learn more, grow more in faith, love God more, and love your neighbor more. It is the journey of faith that begins in love and ends in love.

Frederick Douglass, the American slave turned social activist, said, "If there is no struggle, there is no progress." Your character is formed by the challenges you face and overcome. Your courage grows when you face your fears. Your strength and your faith are built as they are tested in your life experiences.

MY FAITH IN ACTION

I have discovered time and again that when we ask for God's help and then take action, knowing in our hearts that He is watching over us, there is no reason to be fearful. My parents taught me this, mostly in the way they lived each day. They are the greatest examples of faith in action I have witnessed.

Though I arrived on this earth missing, as my mother says, "a few bits and pieces," I am blessed in many, many ways. My parents have always been there for me. They did not coddle me. They disciplined me when I needed it and gave me room to make my own mistakes. Most of all, they are wonderful role models.

I was their first child and definitely a surprise package. Despite doing all the usual maternity tests, my mother's doctor detected no indication that I would come into the world with neither arms nor legs. My mother was an experienced nurse who had assisted in hundreds of deliveries, so she took every precaution during her pregnancy.

Needless to say, she and my father were quite stunned that I arrived without limbs. They are devout Christians. In fact, my father was a lay pastor. My parents prayed for guidance while I underwent many days of testing after my birth.

Like all babies, I did not come with an instruction book, but my parents sure would have welcomed a little guidance. They knew of no other parents who'd raised a child without limbs in a world designed for people with a complete set.

They were distraught at first, as any parents would be. Anger, guilt, fear, depression, despair—their emotions ran away with them for the first week or so. Many tears were shed. They grieved for the perfectly formed child they'd envisioned but did not receive. They grieved, too, because they feared that my life would be very difficult.

My parents could not imagine what plan God had in mind for such a boy. Yet, once they'd recovered from their initial shock, they decided to put their trust in God and then to put their faith in action. They gave up their attempts to understand why God had given them such a child. Instead, they surrendered to His plan, whatever it might be, and then went about raising me as best they could, the only way they could: pouring into me all their love one day at a time.

CUSTOM MADE FOR A PURPOSE

When my parents exhausted all the medical resources in Australia, they sought help for me in Canada and the United States and anywhere else in the world that offered hope and information. They never did uncover a full medical explanation for my condition, though many theories were offered. My brother, Aaron, and sister, Michelle, were born a few years later with the standard package of limbs, so a genetic defect did not appear to be the problem.

After a while, the *why* of my creation became far less important to my parents than the *how* of my survival. How would this boy learn to be mobile without legs? How would he care for himself? How would he go to school? How would he ever support himself as an adult? None of this concerned little baby me, of course. I had no idea that my body wasn't the standard issue. I thought people stared at me because I was so adorable. I also believed I was indestructible and unstoppable. My poor parents could hardly contain their fears as I routinely flung myself like a human beanbag off the couch and onto the floor, over car seats, and around the yard.

You can imagine their concern when they first caught me skateboarding down a steep hill. *Look, Mom, no hands!* Despite their loving efforts to provide me with wheelchairs and other apparatus, I stubbornly developed my own approaches to mobility. The skin on my forehead grew as thick as the soles of most feet because I insisted on raising myself from a prone position by bracing it against walls, furniture, or any other stationary object, and then slowly wriggling my way upright.

To the horror of many innocent bystanders, I also tended to plunge into swimming pools and lakes after I discovered I could swim and remain buoyant by keeping a bit of air in my lungs while paddling about with my little foot. That handy little appendage would prove to be invaluable after an operation was done to separate two fused toes, allowing me to manipulate them with surprising dexterity. With the arrival of cell phones and notebook computers, I could use my foot to type and text, which also proved to be a blessing.

I eventually learned to focus on solutions rather than problems, on doing instead of stewing. I found that when I got rolling on something, there was a snowball effect. My momentum picked up and my problem-solving powers increased. It's said that the universe rewards action, and that certainly has been true for me.

Day by day, God has revealed His plans for me. Your fears and concerns will be diminished too, if you turn them over to Him and act in faith, working on solutions, building momentum, and trusting that God will show you the path.

You will still face challenges and frustrations. They are part of life. Yet when you put your faith in action, you tend to be unstoppable, seeing obstacles as opportunities to learn and grow. Honestly, I may not always welcome challenges. Sometimes when they occur, I want to ask God, "Haven't You given me enough to deal with?" But time and again, I've been able to apply what I've learned and come out the better for the experience, as difficult as it may have been.

I have had so many of these learning opportunities I should be master of the universe by now. As you might imagine, my greatest hurdles came in adolescence, the time in life when we are all trying to figure out who we are and how we fit in—or don't fit in.

Even though I had many friends and was popular in school, there were bullies who tormented me. More than once, cruel comments were thrown my way. Despite my naturally optimistic and determined spirit, I became increasingly aware that I would never look like everyone else, nor would I be able to do all the things that normally configured people can do.

As much as I tried to make jokes about my lack of limbs, I was increasingly tormented by the thought that I would be a burden on those who loved me, because I wouldn't be able to support myself. My other great fear was that I would never be able to marry and have my own family, because no woman would want a husband who couldn't hug her, protect her, or hold their children.

In those adolescent years, I fretted constantly and my thoughts turned dark. I could not imagine why God would create me to suffer such deprivation and loneliness. I wondered if He was punishing me or if He was even aware of me. *Was I a mistake? How can a God who loves all His children be so cruel?*

Between the ages of eight and ten, those darkening thoughts triggered despair and destructive impulses. I began contemplating suicide. I'd find myself plotting to leap off a high ledge or to drown myself in the bathtub, where my parents had no fear of leaving me since I had learned to swim.

Finally, I did make an attempt at suicide in the bathtub when I was ten years old. I tried a couple of times to roll and hold my face under water, but I could not go through with it. I kept thinking of the grief and guilt that would burden my parents for the rest of their lives if I took my own life. I could not do that to them.

At that lowest point I couldn't see that my life had a purpose. If I couldn't support myself and wasn't worthy of love from a woman, what good was I? My fear was that I'd float through life, alone and a burden on my family. My youthful despair was rooted in a lack of faith in myself, in my purpose, and in my Creator. I could not see my path, and so I did not believe it was possible for me to have a purposeful and fulfilling life. Because God had not granted my request for a miracle that would give me arms and legs, I lost faith in Him too.

You may have had a similar experience. Maybe you are dealing with a challenge right now. If so, please understand just how wrong I was and how limited my vision had become because of my loss of faith. I forgot that God does not make mistakes, and He always has a plan for us.

In the years that followed, His plan was slowly revealed to me, and my life unfolded in ways I never dared to dream. My parents encouraged me to reach out to my fellow students and to trust that most would accept me. When I did that, I discovered they were actually inspired by my stories of overcoming my disability. Some even thought I was funny! Their acceptance motivated me to speak to student organizations and church groups. The positive response to my speeches opened my eyes. Over time I realized that one of my purposes was to inspire people to overcome their own challenges and to bring them closer to God, if they were willing.

I came to believe in my own value. My faith in God grew stronger and stronger the more I acted upon it. When I put faith into action and embarked on a career as an international speaker and evangelist, I was rewarded with a joyful and incredibly rewarding life that has taken me around the world, introduced me to millions of people and now *you*!

No Proof Required

You and I cannot see what God has in store for us. That is why you should never believe that your worst fears are your fate or that when you are down, you will never rise again. You must have faith in yourself, in your purpose, and in God's plan for your life. Then you must put fears and insecurities aside and trust that you will find your way. You may not have a clue of what lies ahead, but it's better to act on life than simply let life act on you.

If you have faith, you don't need proof—you live it. You don't need to have all the right answers, just the right questions. No one knows what the future holds. Most of the time, God's plan is beyond our grasp and often beyond even the reach of our imaginations. As a ten-year-old boy, I never would have believed that within the next ten years, God would send me to travel the world to speak to millions of people, inspiring them and leading them to Jesus Christ. Nor could I ever have known that the love of my family would one day be matched and even surpassed by the love of the intelligent, spiritual, fearless, and beautiful young woman who recently became my wife. That boy who despaired at the thought of his future is at peace today as a man. I know who I am, and I take one step at a time, knowing God is on my side. My life is overflowing with purpose and love. Are my days free of worry? Is every day blessed with sunshine and flowers? No, we all know life doesn't work that way. But I thank God for each and every moment that He allows me to walk the path He has set out for me. You and I are here for a purpose. I've found mine, and you should take my story as an assurance that your path awaits you too.

BELIEVING AND ACHIEVING

When you accept on faith that you will find your purpose and then move step by step on the path to discovery, you will find as I have that God's vision of your life is far greater than anything you might imagine. For example, I may never receive the miracle of arms and legs, but I have seen many times that I can be a miracle for someone else. Through my experiences, including the despair that led to my suicide attempt, I can relate to the struggles of others.

I can be the miracle that opens your eyes, inspires you, instills courage in heart, assures you that you are loved, and sends you forward to serve your purpose.

LOVE DRIVES FAITH INTO ACTION

Faith in action comes down to love. I love you so much that I care enough about you to serve you and help you and lend an ear, to inspire you and encourage you. It always comes back to love. We have the power to love without limits, and we need to activate that love, not just to fulfill our purpose, but to play a part in seeing the whole world come to a peace and fulfillment in life. If your journey starts and ends in love, I want to be a part of the God-given love to carry you through.

The apostle Paul said, "If I speak in the tongues of men or of angels, but do not have love, I am only a resounding gong or a clanging cymbal.... If I have a faith that can move mountains, but do not have love, I am nothing."

In a world that can often seem callous and cruel, we tend to lose sight of the fact that God loves us. He sent His Son to pay the price and die for us. He is always there for us. When you know the strength of God, all you want to do is love Him and all those around you. You may forget that sometimes. I know I have. Yet I've found that when I'm most confused about God's plan for me, when I'm seriously struggling to figure out what I should do to serve His purpose, He will place someone in my path or create a situation to reveal that purpose or to test whether I walk the talk. My experience with Felipe Camiroaga is one of the most recent and compelling examples of this.

For many years Felipe was the cohost of a television talk show in Chile that is as popular as *The Oprah Winfrey Show* was in the United States. He and Carolina de Moras hosted Chile's longest-running talk show, *Buenos Dias a Todos,* which translates to "Good Morning, Everyone." The show is the highest rated of all those broadcast on TVN, Chile's state-owned television network. I was invited to appear on that show during my second visit to Chile in September 2011. The interview was supposed to last twenty minutes, which is long for a guest spot, especially when a translator is needed. Yet my visit with Felipe and Carolina went on for forty minutes, which is almost unheard of on such a show. Even better, from my perspective, was the fact that my hosts allowed me to speak at length about what my faith means to me and how I put that faith into action by traveling around the world as an evangelist and inspirational speaker. Felipe seemed intently interested in my message, which surprised me.

I did not know him well, but I was aware of his reputation as perhaps Chile's most high-profile bachelor—a man whose love life had long been the subject of much interest in the media. Many people seemed to think of Felipe merely as a celebrity, but during our interview he asked serious questions about spiritual matters.

He asked me, for example, how I came to know God. I said it requires faith, which is the act of believing in something of which there is no physical proof. I spoke of my faith that Jesus is the path to heaven and eternal life. I also confessed to Carolina and Felipe and their television audience that I am a greedy person: ninety years on this earth is not long enough for me; I want to live forever in heaven. "But there is one thing better than going to heaven and that is to encourage at least one other person to go with me," I said. "That is why I have strength. I keep a pair of shoes in my closet because I believe in miracles, but there is no greater miracle than seeing someone come to God. So pray for faith, and God will help you one day at a time."

As I spoke, a wave of gratitude washed over me. I was grateful for being able to express my faith so openly and at such length on Felipe's television show. I also noticed that Felipe seemed to be emotionally affected by my words. Tears welled up in his eyes. Carolina also seemed to be listening intently.

I'm an evangelist, so naturally I took their interest as license to keep talking. When they asked if there were limits to my faith, I responded that while I cannot say everything is possible, "There are no limits to the joy and peace within me, no matter what happens to me." I wish I could tell people that if they love God, everything will be okay. The truth is that people still suffer. They endure sickness, financial problems, broken relationships, and the loss of loved ones. Tragedies occur in every life, and I believe we are meant to learn from them. My hope is that when people who are in pain see that I have a joyful life, they will think, *If Nick—without arms and legs—is thankful, then I will be thankful for today, and I will do my best.*

I shared with Carolina and Felipe that I'd been through a rough patch a few months earlier (which I will write more about later). "I always know God is there, but He confuses me still at times. It is hard when you go through a valley. Just remember, 'I'm going to learn something in this valley that I would not have otherwise learned, and I am who I am today because of what I have been through,'" I told them.

You, too, may have felt overwhelmed by events and confused about how something could possibly be part of God's plan for you. As I said that day to my television hosts, it's possible to get through even the darkest times by walking in faith one step at a time, knowing that every day, every breath, and every moment is a gift from God, being thankful all the time to Him. "The biggest danger is thinking you don't need God," I said.

All the time I was speaking, I kept marveling at the fact that no one was signaling for my hosts to cut me off, thank me, and send me packing. At one point Felipe brought out a soccer ball and asked me to demonstrate my world-class soccer skills, which, you can imagine, are pretty much limited to head shots and small chips.

To my amazement, they also played my entire music video, which had just been released. Finally, when it came time to end the show, I was so grateful for all they'd given me that I spent five minutes thanking Felipe and Carolina and all their viewers. Then I prayed for them and asked the Holy Spirit to come down, touch their hearts, and give them strength, peace, and the comfort to know that God loves them, has a plan for them, and will always be with them. I also asked Jesus to help us all have faith to believe in Him.

Again, I kept waiting for someone to come on the set with a hook to yank me offstage, but that never happened. Seriously, I was granted so much airtime that day I began to wonder if my parents, cousins, and other big supporters had secretly invaded the studio, commandeered the director's chair, and taken control of the cameras. Later, I would learn that the show's director was a strong Christian and a big fan, and he'd told his crew to just keep rolling. The director was in tears afterward, and he thanked me warmly. They told us that they've never had such a positive immediate feedback of calls, thanking TVN for letting me share my story.

Guided by Faith

My appearance on the morning show with Felipe and Carolina was such a great experience I was still riding high that afternoon when we returned to our hotel. I was wound up, so I turned on some music while casually surfing the Internet. Then the hotel phone rang. It was my interpreter from the show. She said there'd been an accident and I should check the television news right away. An urgent news flash came on, and they showed a photograph of Felipe and a plane crash site. I understand enough Spanish to pick up on the fact that the crash had been on a remote island, and to my horror, Felipe was one of the twenty-one passengers on board, along with several other TVN employees.

Search-and-rescue teams had been dispatched. The crash occurred off the Juan Fernández Islands, hundreds of miles from the coast of Chile, so reports were sketchy. No one yet knew if there were survivors. Felipe was among five TVN employees who'd gone to one of the islands to tape a segment on the rebuilding efforts there since an earthquake and tsunami wiped out the island's main town in February 2010. The news reporters said the Chilean Air Force plane they were aboard had made two attempts to land in bad weather before crashing. Luggage and other debris had been found in the ocean, near the island's landing strip.

As I watched the broadcast about the crash and the search-and-rescue efforts, I felt sick. I had only known Felipe a few hours, yet I could tell he was impacted by our discussion of faith. He seemed genuinely moved when I talked about being greedy for more than a long life on this earth and my desire for eternal life with God. The nature of his questions and the intent look on his face, as well as his emotional response, gave me the sense that this man was searching for a way into a more spiritual life. All I could think about was Felipe and the others on that plane and the suffering of their families and loved ones. I prayed and prayed for them. It was difficult to focus on anything else, but I had been scheduled months earlier to speak the next night to five thousand people, so I had to do some preparation for that, despite the unfolding tragedy.

The media labeled my appearance on his show as Felipe's "last interview," and all the stations were replaying it when not broadcasting the grim reports of the search-and-rescue operation. The hours dragged by without word of survivors. First they found only debris, and then we learned of bodies being discovered one by one but not identified.

Later that afternoon an executive from TVN contacted me and asked if I would come back to the station to lead a live broadcast prayer for those in the crash and their families, friends, and coworkers. I agreed but wondered how I could offer hope to them and also leave room for mourning. We still had not heard if anyone had survived or even if all the passengers had been accounted for. In the televised prayer session on TVN, I noted that when I'd first seen news of the crash, I told someone, "Thank God there is heaven." I had felt sorrow for those who may have died or suffered in the crash, but I took comfort in the belief they would find peace and God's love in the next life. "Heaven is real and God is real, so we have to make sure our walk with Him is real," I said in my message. "We will get through in the same way my parents taught me to live: one day at a time with Christ by our side."

His Plan Revealed

When I completed my spot for the cameras, TVN executives asked me to address their staff of nearly three hundred people. I had to summon all my willpower to compose myself in front of the grieving group who feared they'd lost their coworkers in the crash. I was overcome with emotion too, especially when the woman who had served as my translator on Felipe and Carolina's show came and hugged me, crying. She had considered Felipe a role model whom she admired greatly, and she was very distraught.

After I consoled and prayed with her, a TVN director pulled me aside. "Nick, I want you to know what happened with Felipe after your show yesterday," he said. I was thrown off at first because he seemed almost upbeat in such a somber setting, but when he told me his story, I understood his feelings of joy. This was the same Christian gentleman who'd directed my segment the day before and let my interview go on twice as long as scheduled. He told me that my reading of Felipe that day had been accurate. The television personality had been on a spiritual quest for a long time, trying to find his way to God.

The director said he had often discussed matters of faith with Felipe, in hopes of bringing him to the Lord. Felipe had been growing closer and closer to accepting Jesus into his heart, but he had not yet made the commitment. The director had long ago told Felipe that one day he hoped to become a full-time preacher so he could minister to needy people in Chile. After my appearance on the show, Felipe said that he could finally see the value in that career change.

The director said I might have helped Felipe move a step closer to God just hours before the plane accident. Upon hearing that, I thanked God once again for revealing His plan for me. It is humbling to think that I could be a tool in His hands used to benefit others.

OPPORTUNITIES TAKEN

Later that night, as I was just a few minutes into a speech to five thousand people at Movistar Arena in Santiago, a young woman walked on stage and whispered into my ear that the government had officially announced that the crew and all twenty-one passengers aboard Felipe's airplane had died in the crash.

Times like this can strike us as so unfair. When sent reeling by the death of a friend or loved one, by sickness, broken relationships, or financial crises, you should not blame God. Instead, choose to have faith. Know that He will soothe you with joy, peace, strength, and love.

I mourned the loss of lives, and my heart went out to the families of those killed in the crash. Yet I was grateful that my testimony and response to Felipe's questions during our interview might have helped take Felipe a few steps closer on his path to eternal salvation.

After learning that there were no survivors in the plane crash, I paused briefly, and then shared the news with my audience. Men and women consoled one another. Many sobbed quietly into the shoulders of those next to them. I asked everyone to join me in a prayer for the victims' families and friends, for the people at TVN, and all of Chile, which in recent years had experienced this plane crash, earthquakes, and the mine collapse that had trapped thirty-three miners during my first visit to this beautiful country just a year earlier. I then recounted for my audience the wonderful interview I'd had with Felipe and Carolina just the day before. I told them how generous they were to extend the interview from twenty minutes to forty. And I shared this thought: "I did not know that the first time I met Felipe would be the last."

That is truly a bittersweet thought. Bitter because Felipe and I had made a connection that day and I looked forward to discussing with him my faith in greater depth someday. Now I will not have that opportunity. Yet the sweetness lies in the fact that I did not miss the most important opportunity with Felipe. I am a man of faith, and I acted upon that faith by proclaiming it and sharing my beliefs with Felipe when he inquired. I did not hesitate. I believe my purpose is to bring as many souls to God as I possibly can, and so I acted upon that purpose.

I regret that Felipe and the others aboard that plane are no longer with us, but I have no regrets about my interaction with my television host. In fact, I feel blessed that God allowed me to share my faith.

You should never miss an opportunity to act upon your faith or beliefs because you could be the last person to influence someone, to give him courage, or to inspire him. None of us know when our own time will come to move from this life to the next. That is why you should define your purpose in life. Decide what you know based on facts as well as what you believe based on faith. Then take action to fulfill your purpose according to those convictions. You will never regret living that way.

I put faith and my beliefs out there for Felipe and Carolina and their millions of viewers. I shared with them exactly how I felt and why I felt that way. I admitted that I was not always strong, that I have occasional doubts, and sometimes I am confused. My faith is strong, and it is sometimes hard to see clearly how everything has perfect purpose. But to embrace the journey and believe you are not alone through it is what I try to inspire in others.

I have no regrets about opening up and proclaiming my faith. In whatever purpose you hope to serve, you should do the same. When you put your faith and beliefs into action, you will discover the life for which you were created.

TWO

Rising from a Fall

I AM STILL IN MY TWENTIES, YET I HAVE MANAGED TO BUILD A VERY fulfilling life so far. My nonprofit evangelical organization (Life Without Limbs) and my speaking and inspirational DVD business (Attitude Is Altitude) have taken me around the world to serve others. In the last seven years, I've spoken to more than four million people, making as many as two hundred seventy appearances a year while crisscrossing the globe and visiting forty-three countries.

But in December 2010, I hit a wall.

Sometimes, just as life appears to be flowing your way and you are running at full steam, a serious speed bump rises up directly in your path and *wham!* The next thing you know, friends and family are gathered around your bed, stroking your hair, patting you on the shoulder, and telling you everything will be all right.

Have you been there too? Maybe you are there now, flat on your back, feeling like the old blues song says: "Been down so long it looks like up to me."

I know the feeling all too well. In fact, in my speeches I often encourage my audiences to do whatever it takes to fight back from adversity by demonstrating my method for getting up without arms and legs. I plop down on my belly and then apply my patented forehead-brace-and-crawl move to return to an upright position. I then tell my audience that even when there appears to be no way, there is always a way. Over the years I've built up strong neck, shoulder, and chest muscles from raising myself up in that manner.

There are times though when I struggle to recover from a setback. A major crisis like a serious financial problem, a lost job, a broken relationship, or the loss of a loved one can be difficult for anyone to manage. Even a relatively minor challenge can seem overwhelming if you are already wounded or vulnerable. If you find yourself struggling more than usual with a challenge, my recommended recovery plan is to lean with gratitude on those who care about you, be patient with your tender feelings, do your best to understand the realities versus the emotions at play, and put your faith into action. As hard as it may seem, move forward one step at a time, day by day, knowing that there will be valuable lessons learned and strength gained in each trial. There is a certain peace to be found in knowing that there is a master plan for your life and that your value, purpose, and destiny are not determined by what happens to you but by how you respond.

TURNING ON THE POWER

My approach to applying faith in action in times of crises and extreme challenges has three prongs. First, you need to make internal adjustments to manage your emotions so they don't manage you. This will allow you to take control of your life and respond thoughtfully one step at a time. Second, remind yourself of how you have persevered through adversity in the past and emerged stronger and wiser for the experience. Third, put your faith in action externally by reaching out, not only to seek help and encouragement from others, but to give help and encouragement too. There is healing power in both receiving and in giving.

My recent meltdown sent me reeling for an extended period, longer than any other time in my adult life. The experience reminded me once again that having faith isn't enough: you must live your faith by putting it into action each and every day.

I'm about to bare my soul to you, serving up my initial reaction to a difficult situation as a good example of a bad example. I will share my pain to spare you similar torments. But you have to promise me that you will take this lesson to heart, because this isn't easy to write about. Okay, mate?

Though I would not wish hard times on anyone, major meltdowns seem to be a part of life. I like to believe that rough patches are meant to teach me important things about myself, such as the strength of my character and the depth of my faith. You have probably experienced your own meltdowns, and I'm sure you've taken away lessons learned. Personal, career, or financial crises are all too common and often difficult to recover from emotionally. But if you see hard times as opportunities for learning and growth, you will likely bounce back stronger and quicker. If your despair does not ease within a reasonable amount of time, or if you feel depressed over long periods, please reach out for help either to someone you trust or a counselor. Some forms of emotional trauma require professional help. There is no shame in taking advantage of expert care. Millions of people have been relieved of their severe depression in this way.

Paralyzing sadness, despair, and grief brought on by hard times or tragedies can strike anyone. Unexpected and stressful events can leave us feeling overwhelmed and emotionally beaten, bruised, and battered. It's important that you not isolate yourself in these situations. Allow your family and friends to console you. Be patient with them and with yourself. Healing takes time. Few people can just "snap out of it," so don't expect that to happen. Rather know that you have to work at healing. It's not a passive process. You must flip the switch and tap into whatever power runs through you, including your willpower and the power of your faith.

HEALING OLD WOUNDS

When you find yourself superstressed, highly emotional, and unable to function because of something that has occurred, it is important to separate what has happened *to* you from what is going on *inside* you. We all bear emotional scars from past experiences. Sometimes those scars are not fully healed, so when you hit hard times, the old wounds reopen. The deep pain you feel may be aggravated by past hurts and reawakened insecurities. If you sense that you may be overreacting to a bad situation, or if you feel overwhelmed and unable to cope, you should ask yourself, *Why is this hitting me so hard? Am I reacting this way because of what is actually occurring, or am I reacting so strongly because of what has occurred in the past?*

I was reminded of the importance of analyzing my feelings and their impact on my actions in late 2010. Looking back, I see now that the very rough patch I hit then really wasn't a major calamity. It just seemed that way because I was exhausted spiritually, mentally, and emotionally from working so much and constantly traveling. This was the first time one of my businesses had serious financial challenges. Ironically, the problem that laid me so low arose within my Attitude Is Altitude company, which markets my motivational and inspirational speeches and DVDs. That business had experienced increased demand even during the recession, so I'd hired more people and expanded operations. I thought the company was in good shape, so I was quite surprised when my staff notified me that they were having trouble keeping up with payroll and bills. We'd been doing so well despite the bad economy, but suddenly, big customers who owed us money for DVDs and speaking engagements were either slow to pay or not paying us at all. Money that we'd counted on did not arrive, and that was a big part of the problem.

The other major factor was this bullheaded bloke named Nick Vujicic. I'd long wanted to make a Christian music video as an inspirational item to sell through my business. When business was booming and my first book was hitting bestseller lists around the world, I felt very optimistic about the future. So I decided to make the music video as a product for Attitude Is Altitude. Between the cash flow problem and the music video costs, which were higher than I'd expected, our business fell fifty thousand dollars in debt. We'd been running at 150 mph, and suddenly I had to slam on the brakes. That is no exaggeration. We had seventeen projects underway, and I canceled or postponed nearly all of them. I told the staff we were switching to survival mode. Such problems are common to fast-growing companies, especially when the overall economy is in a recession. Still, this development caught me by surprise. Guilt set in. I'd been so intent on fulfilling my purpose of inspiring and evangelizing to people around the world that I'd overreached. Just because I had the resources and a good idea didn't mean the timing was right. I was operating on Nick's time instead of God's.

When I realized that the company had fallen into debt, I was consumed by the feeling that I'd let down all the people who worked for me and all those who believed in me. Still, the extent of my despair quickly exceeded the magnitude of the problem. I became so overwrought I could barely function, and it wasn't just for a day or two.

My despair went on for more than a month. It took about two more months to pull out of my funk entirely. I lost confidence in myself, and I'm sad to say, I just lost it altogether. I internalized the frustration and shock.

I reverted to that fragile and insecure boy I'd once been. I could not stop the negative thoughts. *Have I wandered away from God's plan for me? Who was I to offer advice, inspiration, and spiritual guidance to people around the world? If I wasn't a speaker and evangelist, what could I be? What value did I have?* I kept flashing back to my worst childhood insecurities. The financial problems, which were really just short-term cash flow issues, reawakened my old fears of being a burden upon my parents and siblings.

As you can imagine, my parents had serious concerns when I first moved to the United States on my own at the age of twenty-four. I was determined to prove my independence and to follow my dream of being an international evangelist and speaker. Since then I'd come a long way in accomplishing my dreams and proving my independence. In fact, my parents had decided to move to the United States so that my father, who is an accountant and wonderful with bookkeeping, could join my business.

The most difficult thing I had to do after learning of the financial problems at Attitude Is Altitude was to call my father and tell him that he was about to join a company that had fallen into debt. He had made the decision to move to the United States without knowing what he was getting into. I was so embarrassed. I felt I'd let him down and disappointed him.

I've always been more of a dreamer and far more impulsive than my father, who is very practical and analytical. He and my mother had warned me before I moved to the United States that I needed to manage my money carefully. I'd messed up just as they were coming to join my business. I also was afraid people would think that my parents were coming to save me, their son with no arms and no legs—and no money!

To make matters even worse, I had hired one of my cousins to work at Attitude Is Altitude so he could learn about starting a business. I was afraid he'd think that he'd apprenticed himself to a loser.

Those nagging thoughts were very difficult to deal with. My old fears of failure and of being a burden assailed me like an angry swarm of insects. I'd been working so hard, and with the release of my first book, I was finally beginning to see the light at the end of the tunnel. And then the light went out.

THE DARK SIDE

Depression set in. I didn't want to leave my bed. Even though I felt like I was in no shape to be offering anyone motivation or inspiration, I had to fulfill several speaking obligations. I'll never forget those appearances because I only got through them with God's grace and mercy. I cried for two hours in despair right before speaking at one motivational seminar. A friend was with me during that crying spell and then attended the speech. He said it was the best talk I'd ever given! I didn't believe him until I saw a recording of it later. I wasn't operating under my own power; God was hard at work that night.

I made it through that appearance, but the next day my despair once again overwhelmed me. I couldn't eat. I couldn't sleep. Anxieties whipsawed me day and night. It was crazy, mate. Strange things happened to me. When I was a kid, I had a nervous habit of biting my lip. I started doing that again! What was that about? I'd toss and turn all night and then wake up with a sore and swollen lip and my chest and stomach in knots.

Strangest of all, four or five days passed before I could even think about praying. I'm a habitual prayer. My inability to pray scared me. When days went by without a single prayer passing my lips, I worried for my soul as well as my sanity.

My mental paralysis left me unable to make even the most minor decisions. Normally, I fly through the day making dozens of important decisions regarding my schedule, projects, and other business. During this troubled time I couldn't decide whether to get out of bed or whether I should try to eat.

My lethargy was humbling, to say the least. It was as though I'd become another person. One day, a group of employees and contractors for Attitude Is Altitude gathered at my house, and I found myself trying to explain the transformation.

"The Nick you've known, the big dreamer and overachiever, is gone," I told them tearfully. "He's done. I'm so sorry I let you down." Those closest to me—my parents, my brother and sister, my friends, and my advisors— did their best to console me at first, and then, as I continued to wallow in despair, they rallied around, trying to snap me out of it. They held, hugged, and reassured me. My ministry staff members were ever gracious, giving me space but sharing jokes, smiles, and hugs to encourage me. They even quoted me to myself. "Nick, you always say that as long as you can look up, you can get up. Watch your DVDs and videos, remind yourself of what you already know!" they suggested. "There is a lesson in this. You will get through this, and you will be stronger than ever. God has a reason!"

It was so surreal to have someone quote my own words to me to try to lift my spirits. Yet they were right. I just needed to be reminded of the same things I tell others all the time. I was the poster child for someone whose faith was missing in action. My guilt and shame over the cash problems of my business left me questioning my value, my purpose, and my path. I didn't doubt God's perfection. I just couldn't access my belief system because of the despair.

Another who tried to help me was a Dallas friend, Dr. Raymund King, who is both an attorney and a physician. He had arranged for me to speak at a medical seminar, and I didn't want to disappoint him. But when I arrived, he could see I was emotionally and physically drained.

"You have to take care of yourself first," he said. "Without your health you will lose all you've worked for." Gently, he took me aside and counseled me about keeping my priorities straight, and then he prayed a simple prayer with me and hugged me. It had been a struggle just to get there, but Dr. King's caring words really hit home. It may have been the best motivational speech I've ever received. His words stayed with me because he obviously was concerned for me.

His little talk reminded me of one my father gave me when I was just six years old. I had a tendency to be a little reckless and over the top when it came to throwing myself around. I'd banged myself up clowning around with a classmate who offered me a bite of a banana while I was sitting in my wheelchair. I lurched forward to chomp on it like a monkey, and in the process I tipped forward in my chair, crashed to the ground, and banged my head so badly I blacked out momentarily.

My father's concern was touching, and I'll always remember his words: "Son, you can always get another banana, but we can't get another Nicky, so you need to be more careful."

Like my father, Dr. King urged me to examine my actions and their impact on my life. I had been driving myself because I thought the success of all my endeavors depended on me when, in fact, I should have trusted in God and relied more on His strength and His will and His timing.

That lack of humility and faith led to my meltdown and the loss of joy in my life for a brief season. I began to see my speaking engagements as a duty rather than as my purpose. Because I was afraid I would not be able to provide what mourning students needed, I even turned down a request to speak at a high school where there had been a student suicide. I cried after refusing that opportunity because speaking is my passion and helping others is the source of my joy.

LESSONS REVEALED

I wish I could tell you that one morning I woke up with a clear head and a renewed spirit, jumped out of bed, and announced, "I'm baaaaack!" Sorry, it didn't happen that way for me, and if you go through a similar rough period, you may not pop right out of it either. Just know that better days are ahead, and this too shall pass.

My comeback played out in small steps, day by day, over a couple of months. I hope your recovery comes more quickly, but there are benefits to a gradual revival. As the fog of despair slowly lifted, I was grateful for every ray of light that came through. Even more, once my head began to clear of the self-defeating thoughts, I appreciated the time I was given to reflect and contemplate my plunge into the abyss.

It should go without saying that putting your faith into action is not a passive exercise. You have to actively and willfully take the necessary steps to locate and move along the path God designed for you. When you fall off the path, as I did in this instance, at some point you have to ask yourself what happened, why it happened, and what you need to do to resume your journey of faith and purpose.

The worst times that test your faith can be the best times for renewing it and putting it into action. A wise soccer coach once told me that he values losing as much as he values winning, because losing reveals weaknesses and failings that have probably been there all the time and need to be addressed if the team is to experience long-term success. Losses also motivate his players to work on the skills they need to master in order to win.

When your life is going well, the natural tendency is not to pause and assess it. Most of us only take the time to examine our lives, our careers, and our relationships when we aren't getting our desired results. In every setback, failure, and defeat, there are valuable lessons to be learned and even blessings to be unlocked.

In the early days of my despair over my company's debt, I wasn't much in the mood for seeking out the lessons. But they found me over time, and the blessings revealed themselves too. I don't like to reflect on that period, but I force myself to revisit it because new layers unfold and more lessons emerge on every visit. I encourage you to look for the learning points in each of your own challenges. You may be tempted to put hard times behind you and out of your mind. No one likes feeling vulnerable. It's certainly no fun recalling how I wallowed in my misery, held pity parties, and grossly overreacted to what proved to be a temporary setback.

Yet one of the best ways to take the pain out of past experiences is to replace the hurt with gratitude. The Bible tells us that "all things work together for good to them that love God, to them who are the called according to his purpose."

My uncle Batta Vujicic, who has faced difficult challenges in his real estate business, has helped me many times by gently repeating his mantra of faith: "It's all positive." My young cousins put their own spin on it, say-ing, "Dude, it's all good in the hood!"

PERCEPTIONS VERSUS REALITY

During my meltdown I experienced something that you may have noticed in your own trials. As stress opened up old wounds and insecurities, my perception of what was going on became much worse than the reality of the situation. One tip-off that your response is out of sync with your actual situation is the use of inflated and exaggerated descriptions such as:

This is killing me.

I will never recover from this!

This is absolutely the worst thing that's ever happened to me.

Why does God hate me?

And there is the always popular: *My life is destroyed*—forever!

I will not admit to actually saying any of those silly things during my recent tribulations, but some people who were in my vicinity might have thought they heard similar lamentations. (Or worse!)

Once again, I am honored to provide you with a good example of a bad example in my own behavior. The wielding of such over-the-top language should have served as a warning that my despair was excessive.

Here are my perceptions of what was going on: *I'm a failure! I'm going to go bankrupt! My worst fears are realized! I'm not able to support myself! I'm a burden on my parents! I'm not worthy of love!*

Here is the reality of what was occurring: My business was experienc-ing a temporary cash-flow problem during an economic recession. We were fifty thousand dollars in the red, which was not good. But it certainly was not an overwhelming deficit, given the prospects for growth in the global demand for our products and services. I majored in accounting and financial planning in college, and economics was part of the curriculum. I knew about supply and demand and cash flow, but what I knew was clouded by what I felt.

You may have experienced a similar sensation of being so overwhelmed, even though your actual situation was not nearly as devastating as it seemed. Our vision can become impaired by our feelings, and in the midst of despair, it can be very difficult to look at things realistically.

MAINTAINING PERSPECTIVE

One of the lessons I learned is that you have to keep things in perspective, even when you are in the middle of a personal crisis. Fear breeds fear and worry builds upon worry. You can't stop the feelings of grief, remorse, guilt, anger, and fear that wash over you during difficult times, but you can recognize them as pure emotional responses, and then manage them so that they don't dictate your actions.

Maintaining perspective requires maturity, and maturity comes with experience. I had never been through a situation like this, and because I was physically drained by all my traveling, I had a difficult time handling this crisis in a mature manner.

My father and other older-and-wiser friends and family members tried to help me by telling me they'd been through similar or worse experiences and had bounced back. As I mentioned, my uncle Batta is in the real-estate development and property management business in California. You can imagine the ups and downs he has seen. An operating deficit of fifty thousand dollars is small change in his business, and he tried to tell me that it was not a crippling debt for mine either.

Still, as much as I would like to learn from other people's advice and mistakes, for the longest time I seemed to need to make my own blunders before I gained any true wisdom. I've now resolved to be a better student. If you and I can learn just one lesson from every person we know, how much wiser would we be? How much time, effort, and money would we save?

When our loved ones and friends give advice, why can't we listen, absorb the lesson, and make the necessary adjustments? You only increase your stress by thinking you have to fix things *right now*! True, some crises demand immediate action, but that action can include a step-by-step, one-day-at-a-time approach to problem solving. A member of my advisory board once made this point when he said, "Nick, do you know the best way to eat an entire elephant? One bite at a time."

HUMILITY DELIVERED

For years my father, the accountant, had been telling me to be careful with my finances, to save more than I spend, and to always have a budget in mind whenever I started a new project.

I tuned him out. *I'm a risk taker; he's more conservative. We just have two different personalities. This is not the time to save; this is the time to invest and plant.* Humility is an interesting virtue because if you don't have it, sooner or later it's given to you. Imagine how humbling it was for me to have to accept my father's offer of a fifty-thousand-dollar personal loan to bail out my business! That hurt, but it was a self-inflicted pain. Proverbs 16:18 tells us, "Pride goes before destruction, and a haughty spirit before a fall." I'm pretty sure if you open your Bible to that chapter and verse, you will now see a photograph of me!

In reflecting upon my meltdown, I realized that my humility had been lacking in several areas of my life. Why is humility important to someone going through a crisis? First of all, you may feel embarrassed if your situation is due to a mistake or a failure. In other words, you've been humbled. Getting mad, crying, or giving up won't change that, and responding with negative emotions will probably only make you feel worse and drive people away from you.

My suggestion is that you embrace your newfound humility. Some batters react angrily to striking out. They break their bats over their knees, throw their helmets at the water boy, and kick dents into the dugout wall. Other batters humbly accept that striking out is part of the game, and they remember not to swing at the same pitches next time. So being humbled isn't such a bad thing if you learn from the experience. In fact, there are those who believe that the truest path to enlightenment is through humility.

When I was younger, I developed a strong aversion to asking anyone for help. It's a very humbling thing to have to ask those around you to help you eat or to lift you into a chair or to take you into the rest room. I didn't like being humbled. There were certain benefits and rewards to becoming more independent by finding ways to do things for myself. I'm not saying it's all bad, but my willful self-reliance sometimes led me to manipulate and even bully people into helping me. Instead of just asking for help, I'd wrangle favors from people, like my poor brother, Aaron, whom I often treated like a caregiver instead of a brother. Sorry, Aaron!

From time to time God would have to restore my humility. It had not dawned on me that sometimes I was very selfish, impatient, and proud. At times I felt like I deserved special treatment. But I have asked Aaron for forgiveness, and even though we don't see each other a lot because of distance, he is my best friend, whom I admire and respect a great deal. I am so surprised that when he was big enough to do so, he didn't just put me in a cabinet and lock me in. I deserved it sometimes.

I came to see this dark period as another of those humbling reminders meant to put me back on course. I had been acting as though I had to carry the entire burden of all our operations on my shoulders. That was an arrogant and impossible approach, and it showed that my faith in God and those around me was not shining through.

Moses, the great prophet and leader, was the most humble man on the face of the earth. He knew that you cannot be a leader if no one is willing to follow and work alongside you. An arrogant person does not ask for help and thus is helpless. An arrogant person claims to know everything and thus is clueless. A humble person attracts helpers *and* teachers.

I once heard a father tell his son, a recent college graduate, that he should approach the first day of his job with a proper attitude: "Don't try to show them what you know. Instead, show them how much you want to learn."

If you find yourself overwhelmed by a crisis in your life, you may have to humble yourself and ask for help, and that is a good thing. None of us can accomplish our dreams without the help of others. Is it more important for you to feel superior and self-sufficient than to accomplish your dreams within a community of supporters?

Humility also fosters gratitude and appreciation, which are forces for healing and happiness. No single human being is more valuable than another. Somewhere I forgot that fact. The pride that led to my downfall clouded my memory and my vision. I had to remind myself that God doesn't love me because my business shows a profit or because I speak two hundred seventy times a year around the world. He loves me because He created me. He loves me for me, and He loves you for you.

I still believe that those projects and dreams that I had to abandon during that difficult time were put in my heart for a reason. I believe that God gave me a clear vision and all I needed to plant them, but I should have prayed more to determine what His timing was instead of going ahead on my own. It's not important who does the planting or who does the watering. What's important is that God makes the seed grow.

While we may not always be faithful to God, He is always faithful to us. I had not been consciously putting my faith into action each and every day. I resolved to do that—not just to pray, but to move forward with perspective, patience, humility, courage, and confidence daily, knowing that where I am weak, God is strong, and what I lack, God will provide.

Letting Faith Shine

Faith, whether it is faith in yourself and your purpose or faith in your Creator, is a powerful beacon, but you have to let its light shine. You cannot allow it to be dimmed by neglect. Sometimes, you may feel like you have faith, but there is no light showing. I realized I had to let my faith shine. From a different perspective my faith had become like a car with the transmission in neutral. It was there, but it was not engaged. Having faith in yourself and your abilities is critical, but you must also have patience, humility, and the understanding that you cannot do anything without the help of others and, in the end, all credit goes to God.

Nothing will bring you down faster than living without purpose or losing track of whatever you are most passionate about: the gift that gives you joy and makes your life meaningful. I lost track of my purpose to inspire and encourage others while spreading the message of faith. I was trying to do too many other things to build my business and charity. When I strayed from my true purpose, it was as if someone unplugged my power cord.

If you feel yourself sliding into despair, drained of energy, and depleted of faith, ask yourself, *What matters most to me? What gives me joy? What drives me and gives my life meaning? How can I get back to that?*

You and I were put on this earth to serve something greater than our narrow interests. When our focus becomes self-centered instead of God-centered, we lose our greatest source of power. Our God-given talents are meant to benefit others. When we use them for that greater purpose, we put faith into action to fulfill His plan for us. We make a difference in this world that helps prepare us for the next.

BEDRIDDEN BUT PURPOSEFUL

I noted earlier that my meltdown left me serving as a good example of a bad example, so you might say that I did at least serve *some* purpose as a demonstration of faith gone inactive. Now I'd like to share with you the story of someone who is a great example of a *good* example of faith in action—one of the best I've encountered. In fact, I dedicated my first book to him, but I saved his story for this one.

I first learned of Phil Toth of La Jolla, California, through my mum when we still lived in Australia. My mother had heard of Phil and his Christian website through our church. She showed me his site, and I found his story of faith in action deeply moving. When Phil was just twenty-two years old, he woke up one day and had trouble speaking. At first his family thought he was joking, because he liked to tease and have fun, but then he also experienced dizziness and fatigue that alarmed everyone. For nearly two years his doctors couldn't determine what was wrong, but they finally diagnosed him with amyotrophic lateral sclerosis (ALS), which is often called Lou Gehrig's disease.

The life expectancy for one with this incurable disease, which destroys the motor nerve cells in the brain and spine and causes muscles to deteriorate, is usually two to five years. Initially, Phil's doctors told him that his case was advancing so quickly that he might not survive another three months. Instead, Phil lived for five years, and I think it was because he did not focus on his suffering. He focused instead on encouraging others to pray and trust God. Phil dealt with his deadly illness by celebrating life and reaching out to help others, even though he could not lift his arms or legs from his bed.

ALS is both wickedly cruel and extremely painful. Within a few years, Phil was bedridden and unable to do much for himself. His large circle of loving family and friends provided constant care. Even his voice was affected, making it difficult for people to understand him.

Despite his pain and suffering, Phil remained deeply devoted to his Christian faith, and beyond that he even found a way to put his faith into action so that he could reach out to console and inspire others who were suffering debilitating and deadly illnesses. By God's grace, with all his physical challenges, Phil created the website that my mother discovered through the church. Here is part of the message he posted about his illness and the impact it had on his faith:

> I thank God for leading me through this! It has brought me closer
> to God [it would be worth it if this is all it did], it also caused me
> to reevaluate my life and see if I'm in the faith, caused me to experi-
> ence the love of my brothers and sisters in Christ, near and far.
> Taught me to depend fully on the Word of God, my knowledge
> of the Word increased, as well as maturing in faith. My family

and friends are a lot closer now. Additionally I've been learning
a lot more about health, nutrition, and taking care of my body.
The benefits of my situation are endless.

At my mother's urging, I went to Phil's home in 2002 to meet him
during a trip to the United States. I'd had a cousin suffer through an incurable disease, and I was prepared for the worst. But when I entered Phil's
room, Phil gave me a beautiful and welcoming smile that changed my
life. I will never forget that day. Despite his pain and suffering, Phil did not
retreat into a corner to feel sorry for himself. His strength and courage
touched and inspired me.

Phil and his family never gave up hope for a miracle, even as he prepared himself to be with God in heaven. By the time I met him, ALS had
taken his ability to speak. He could communicate only by blinking through
the alphabet, which he did with amazing patience and grace. He'd found a
way to use laser technology that allowed him to talk to his computer, and
he used it to create a Christian newsletter that had more than three hundred subscribers at one point.

His determined effort to put his faith into action while unable to speak
and while confined to his bed motivated me to begin my own ministry a
few weeks later. From that day forward, whenever I felt discouraged, I
thought of Phil Toth. If he could continue to make a difference and serve
others in his condition, I had no excuse. About a year later I had the honor
of being at his bedside when Phil moved from this life to the next, and
though I mourned his departure from earth, I felt humbled to witness a
general in God's army go home. I only hope that you and I can show the
same determination, courage, and grace while staying in faith and acting
upon it so that we can be a blessing to others.

THREE

Matters of the Heart

I FOUND THE LOVE OF MY LIFE IN A CROWD OF PEOPLE HIGH ATOP THE Bell Tower at Adriatica. While it looks like one of those ancient structures found in old European villages, this stone tower is actually a unique office building in McKinney, Texas, a suburb of Dallas. I was there in April 2010 to speak, but I had some trouble focusing on my talk that day after locking on to the most beautiful, wise, and warm eyes I'd ever seen.

You may think this "love at first sight" story is a cliché, but if this is what being a cliché feels like, believe me, mate, I'm okay with it. As a Christian, I follow the lessons from the Bible. This one is drawn from the Song of Songs: "You have captured my heart, my treasure, my bride. You hold it hostage with one glance of your eyes."

If you follow my website, blog, tweets, or Facebook page, you likely have learned that my heart was captured that day by the wonderful Kanae

Miyahara. We became engaged in July 2011, and we were married in February 2012, just after I finished writing this book.

There are several reasons I want to share with you the story of how Kanae and I met and fell in love. The biggest is that so many people of all ages come to me with questions and stories about their own relationship challenges—junior high kids, teenagers, college students, young adults, middle-agers, seniors, singles, and marrieds. The details of their stories vary, but the central themes are universal: each of them wants to love and be loved in return.

- *Nick, I'm afraid no one will ever love me.*
- *How do I know this is the right person for me?*
- *Why don't my relationships last?*
- *Can I trust this person?*
- *What does love feel like?*
- *I've been hurt so many times I'm afraid to try again.*
- *I'm alone and happy. Is there something wrong with me?*

Matters of the heart have confounded, distressed, and fulfilled males and females since Adam and Eve were banished from the Garden of Eden. The powerful yearning of the heart is one of the most essential human needs. Yet when we look for love, we open ourselves not only to being loved but also, unfortunately, to being hurt. So there is a decision you have to make: you can give up on love and never find it, which seems like a waste of a good life, or you can keep trying.

I put my heart on the line and came away bruised more than once. I was hurt, embarrassed, angry, and sometimes I felt like a complete fool. But I got over it. Each and every time I eventually decided that the only way to find what I was looking for was to put faith into action and keep trying.

You may have had similar heartbreaks. Few of us who choose to seek love survive unscathed. My advice is to consider your failed attempts as nothing more than tests: situations that build your strength to love even more when the right person comes along. As long as you remain open to love, love can happen. If you build a wall around your heart, it won't.

I certainly struggled for many years with feelings of insecurity and loneliness. As someone who is two arms and two legs short of the standard-issue Prince Charming, I feared rejection and often despaired that I would never find someone to share my dream of having a family. I've often spoken and written of my youthful fears that no woman would want me because I cannot hold her hand or hug her.

I grew up, as most men do, with the traditional image of a husband as the provider and protector in a marriage, so the last thing I ever wanted a woman to think was that she would need to care for me instead of simply being my wife and partner in life.

Concerns about finding love are by no means unique to me or other people with physical disabilities. Everyone has insecurities and fears about relationships. Yet I urge you to never give up on love. I found the perfect woman for imperfect me. We know we each have our flaws, but we see ourselves as perfectly matched. (One wise-guy friend who knows us both too well said, "I'm glad you found each other. Why waste two other perfectly good people?")

Now, some people prefer to remain single, and there is nothing wrong with that if it makes you happy and fulfilled. But if it is in your heart to share your life with another person, I assure you there is someone for you if you put your faith into action in matters of the heart. To do that, you first must accept these four basic tenets:

1. You are a child of God. He created you. You may see yourself as imperfect, but God does not. You were made according to His

plan. If you treat others with respect and kindness, if you try to do the right things and to make the most of your gifts, you will be worthy of love.

2. To be loved by others, you must first love yourself. If you find it difficult to love yourself, then you have work to do before you can expect anyone else to sign on to a relationship with you.

3. If you come from love, there is no need to look for it. Put yourself out there by opening your heart to others. Listen to what they say and also to what they feel. Prepare to give your love as a caring, honest, and trustworthy person, and you will surely receive it in equal doses.

4. You cannot give up on love. You may try to bury your feelings, and you may harden your heart as a protective measure, but you were created out of love and it is part of your life force. God does not want you to squander the love you have. Know that broken relationships prepare you for the one that will last. So stay in faith, and remain open to one of God's greatest gifts.

GOD'S LOVE FOR YOU MAKES YOU LOVABLE

As I noted in chapter 1, there was a time early in my life when I felt that if I really was a child of God, I must have been the one child He did not love. I could not understand why a loving God would create me without arms and legs. I even thought God was punishing me or that He must have hated me. *Why else would He make me so different from most other people?* I wondered also why God would create a child who would be a burden to good Christians like my parents.

For a brief time I shut God out of my life because I was angry. I could not accept that He loved me until I realized that everything He does has a purpose. I read a Bible passage in which God used a blind man to teach a lesson. He healed his blindness "that the works of God should be revealed in him." In reading that passage in John 9, I had a revelation. *If God had a purpose for a blind man, He must have one for me too.*

I found God's purpose for me over time, and I realized that I am indeed a beloved child of God, even if He didn't give me arms and legs. The same holds true for you. I had issues. You may have your own. You may have insecurities and imperfections. Don't we all? You may not understand what God has in mind for you. I certainly didn't for the longest time, but when I read of the blind man in the Bible, I put my faith into action. I saw that God had a purpose for the sightless man. I was blind to my own purpose, but my faith allowed me to accept that one day I would find the path God had laid out for me.

The Bible says whoever does not love does not know God, because God is love. Know that you are God's creation and that He loves you just as He loves all who stay in faith.

LOVING FROM THE INSIDE OUT

Once I accepted that God loved me and had a purpose for me, my self-image changed and so did my attitude and my actions. It didn't happen overnight, but over time I stopped avoiding my classmates in school and around town. I no longer went to the music room so I wouldn't have to interact with them during lunch hours. I quit hiding behind the bushes on the playground. My parents had encouraged me to speak up instead of waiting for other kids first to reach out to me. I finally emerged from my shell, and I discovered that once people knew me, they accepted me and found me inspiring. More important, I accepted myself.

When I kept to myself out of a fear of rejection, no one could get to know the real Nick. I felt sorry for myself, and that's all others could feel for me. But when I shared my victories with my classmates, they celebrated them too. Once I opened up to their curiosity and questions about my lack of limbs, talked openly with them, and laughed with them, they became my friends.

Their respect bolstered my self-image and in turn gave me the confidence to be more outgoing. I realized that being different physically was only as limiting as I allowed it to be. There were some things I could not do, but I often surprised others and myself by finding ingenious ways to overcome challenges. I skateboarded, swam, and excelled in many of my classes, especially mathematics and—surprise—speech!

When I understood my own value, I valued others more. They returned my appreciation for them by appreciating me. That's the message contained in the Bible when we're told to love our neighbors as we love ourselves. If you love and accept yourself, you will become more loving and accepting of others. You create an environment in which friendship and love for others can be nurtured.

You attract what you put out. If you have no respect for yourself, do you think others will respect you? If you don't love yourself, can others love you? Of course not. But if you are comfortable in your own skin, others will take comfort in your presence. If you make others feel good about themselves because of your positive, encouraging, accepting, and inspiring presence, I believe love will find you.

When I speak at schools and church gatherings for young people, I always tell them that God loves them just as they are. I tell them they are beautiful and that they need to appreciate themselves as much as God does. Those are simple words. Yet every time I say them, the tears start flowing. Why is that? It's because young people especially think they must fit in or be cast out. Too often they feel it's necessary to have a certain look, certain clothing, certain physical attributes, certain this or that to be accepted. But that's not true. God accepts us as we are.

You are a beautiful child of God. If the Father of us all—the Creator of the universe—loves you, then you must love yourself as well.

GIVE LOVE TO RECEIVE IT

Now, maybe someone you loved and trusted broke your heart. I know it's little consolation, but many others, including me, have gone through this truly awful and humbling experience. But a breakup and betrayal does not make you unworthy. A failed relationship only means that it was the wrong relationship for you. I know that right now you may find it difficult to see why things went wrong, but someday you will understand. In the meantime do not make the mistake of shutting down your ability to love and be loved.

For a time I didn't trust God to make a match for me. I was lonely and tried to push friendships into relationships even when my feelings were not reciprocated. Kanae taught me the beauty of a true loving relationship in which both people are all-in. Loneliness can make you feel that you should settle for a relationship that may be comfortable but lacks the spark of love. But you should not compromise on love. Instead, believe in it. In the Bible, Jesus commands us to love as He loves: "Love one another; as I have loved you, that you also love one another."

Understand that there are many single people with fulfilling and joyous lives. I know unmarried people whose lives are complete with the love of God. I had a strong desire to be married and one day to have a family, but over time I put it in God's hands. I left it to His will to decide whether I would remain single or not.

Okay, I admit that I did pray to God to make Kanae love me, but she was praying that I loved her too. Of course, I didn't know that at the time. It's better to ask the Lord to help you find the one whom He wants you to be with. Pray: *Lord, take my feelings for this person away if it is not Your will* or *If this is the person You want for me, please let us love each other according to Your plan.*

NEVER GIVE UP ON LOVE

You may have tried and lost before. Maybe you've had relationships that did not work out. Consider them preparatory courses for the real thing. I've had failed relationships. I've put my heart out there only to discover that the other person was more interested in a friendship than romance—or worse, neither one! As painful as those breakups and rejections were, I refused to give up on love and loving. It's just too important. Without love we are nothing.

The Bible makes this very clear in 1 Corinthians 13: "If I speak in the tongues of men or of angels, but do not have love, I am only a resounding gong or a clanging cymbal. If I have the gift of prophecy and can fathom all mysteries and all knowledge, and if I have a faith that can move mountains, but do not have love, I am nothing. If I give all I possess to the poor and give over my body to hardship that I may boast, but do not have love, I gain nothing."

For many years I prayed and prayed and prayed for a woman who would truly love me. Did I ever feel discouraged? Yes! Did I sometimes think of giving up and joining the French Foreign Legion? (Well, I do like the uniforms, but the whole marching and shooting thing might present challenges.)

The important point here is that I did not give up, and I encourage you to never give up on love either. Put your faith in action. Pray for God's guidance, focus on being the best person you can be, and open your heart to the possibilities and opportunities that will come to you.

I would not wish loneliness, rejection, or a broken heart on anyone. I hope your path to love and marriage is smoother than mine, yet I have come to understand that the trials I endured prepared me to fully appreciate the joy I've found. God didn't want me to discover my true love until I was mature enough to appreciate and nurture it.

Scripture tells us that of the three spiritual gifts—faith, hope, and love—"the greatest of these is love." This greatest gift is one that we can fully experience with another person when we are physically, emotionally, and spiritually mature. Like most young men, I thought I was prepared for love as a teenager, but I see now that there were experiences God wanted me to have. He sent me across the world several times to speak to millions of people and to see incredible beauty and splendor as well as crippling poverty.

God even allowed me to have relationships that went wrong so that I would fully appreciate the one that would be exactly right. He allowed my heart to be broken so that I would truly appreciate the completeness of love. The end of one particular relationship was painful beyond words, and the breakup confirmed every fear I'd had about rejection. Not to sound too pathetic, but I was a bit of a lost puppy after that experience. I spent several years struggling to rebuild my self-confidence and to build another relationship. I made some good friends with some wonderful women, but I was often lonely and yearned for a deeper, lasting partnership.

You may right now be feeling unloved and lonely, but consider that maybe, just maybe, this time of trial is your preparation for many years of blessings. I know to some that may sound highly optimistic or hopelessly naive, and there were times in my life when I probably felt the same way. But now my once-empty cup has been filled to a level that I never knew existed, thanks to faith in action.

The Eyes of Love

Kanae and her older sister, Yoshie, came to my speech at the Bell Tower at Adriatica with my friend Tammy, who is also a speaker and author, and her husband, Mark. The sisters were then working sporadically as nannies for the couple, but since they were more like family, Tammy had invited them to meet me. Kanae and Yoshie have exotic looks because their mother is Mexican and their father, who sadly passed away, was Japanese. They are both striking, but while speaking that day I had a clear view of Kanae, and I could not take my eyes off her. I could hardly concentrate on what I was saying.

After my speech, I stuck around to talk with members of the audience. Kanae and Yoshie came with Tammy to say hello, and I was very happy to meet them. In fact, when they tried to walk away to make room for other people wanting to speak with me, I told them to stay close so we could get to know one another.

Whenever I had a break, I'd try to get in a few words with them. The more I chatted with Kanae, the more I wanted to whisk her away and find out all there was to know about this enchanting girl who seemed so self-assured and kindhearted.

Finally, as they were preparing to leave, I made a bold move.

"Let me give you my e-mail address so we can stay in touch," I said to Kanae.

"Oh, that's okay, I'll get it from Tammy," she replied.

I really wanted to establish a line of communication with her so that I didn't miss the opportunity to get to know her better. Part of me wanted to beg and plead: *I want to give you my e-mail myself so I'll be sure you have it!*

That's what I wanted to say, but my father had instilled in me that real men do not beg. I took Dad's advice and played it as cool as I could, given my instant infatuation with this enthralling young woman.

"Okay, that's fine. Let's stay in touch," said Mr. Cool.

Kanae and Yoshie then left with Tammy and Mark.

My friends and I were just a few miles down the road when Tammy sent me a text message: "What did you think?"

"She is one of the most beautiful women of God I've ever met, inside and out," I texted back. "She literally took my breath away!"

So much for playing it cool.

This all happened on a Sunday. I flew home to California on Monday, hoping I would hear from Kanae the next day, if not sooner. Maybe I did check my e-mail as soon as the plane landed, and perhaps I kept checking it every ten minutes all day long to see if she'd sent me a message. (Have you seen her? Can you blame me?)

TWITTERPATED

Isn't it crazy how our hearts rule our minds and our actions in these situations? You can be fourteen years old or sixty-four years old—your age doesn't matter. When sparks fly, the reaction is always the same: you can't focus on anything other than trying to figure out how to be with the person who lit your fuse.

This love-struck state of mind is captured in the classic Disney movie *Bambi* when a wise old owl explains to Bambi and his woodland friends that with the arrival of each spring, young males and females of all species can become "twitterpated."

"Nearly everybody gets twitterpated in the springtime," the owl said. "You're walking along, minding your own business.... All of a sudden you run smack into a pretty face.... You begin to get weak in the knees. Your head's in a whirl. And then you feel light as a feather, and before you know it, you're walking on air. And then you know what? You're knocked for a loop, and you completely lose your head.... And that ain't all. It can happen to anyone."

I was *definitely* twitterpated by Kanae. I could not stop thinking about her. The fact that she had not e-mailed me right away was driving me as mad as a cut snake. *Was I wrong? She looked at me like she was feeling the same way. I can't be wrong. There was something going on between us. Wasn't there?*

Days passed. Then weeks. No e-mails from Kanae. Neither a peep nor a tweet.

She seemed to have moved on and forgotten me. I could not think of anything else. I've had crushes on women before, but this was beyond that. Her beauty was undeniable, but she seemed to have so much character, such warmth and faith, and then there was her fearless energy. For Yoshie's twenty-sixth birthday, she and Kanae went skydiving? Skydiving!

I couldn't believe that God would place this dynamic woman in my life, strike up such powerful sparks, and then have her disappear. So I asked Him: *Why would You put her in front of me if You didn't want us to be together? Why would you let me be so distracted from my work for You if there wasn't something important going on between her and me?*

Then, after another week with no word from Kanae, I had a stern talk with myself: *Nick, you did it again. You made up your mind that this girl felt the same for you as you did for her, but you were just dreaming. When will you ever learn?*

I was bummed out that Kanae hadn't contacted me and disappointed in myself for being such a silly mug. I'd turned into a lovesick twelve-year-old just because a pretty, unsuspecting girl had been nice to me.

Nearly three months went by. I thought of Kanae often, but her lack of communication convinced me that nothing romantic was going to happen with her. My male pride had taken another hit. I had to let it go.

COMPETITION OF THE HEART

In July I had another speaking engagement in Dallas. As usual I would be staying with Tammy and Mark, who lived nearby, and I can't deny that I hoped Kanae would be babysitting then. But I also cautioned myself not to get my hopes up. She hadn't e-mailed me, after all. Obviously, she had not felt the same sparks for me that I'd felt for her. I had to back off and stay in control of my feelings. *Guard your heart! Stay cool, mate!*

Our plane had barely touched down before I found myself texting Tammy. "Is everyone there?" I asked, trying not to be obvious.

"Yoshie and I are here cooking lasagna for you," Tammy texted back.

"Great!" wrote Mr. Cool. "How about Kanae?"

I swear, those words typed themselves on my smartphone, which is sometimes too smart for my own good. Okay, so I'm weak when it comes to matters of the heart. I couldn't help myself. But the answer was even worse than I'd feared.

"Kanae is here, but she's out riding bikes with her boyfriend," Tammy said.

I seriously thought Tammy was joking, so I brushed off that comment.

We arrived at Tammy's house, and sure enough Yoshie and she were in the kitchen, working on the lasagna. I took a seat and we chatted for a few minutes before ol' Lovesick Nick kicked in again.

"So, really, where is Kanae?" I asked meekly.

Tammy put down her bowl of freshly made pasta. Both she and Yoshie gave me puzzled looks.

"She *really* is riding bikes with her boyfriend, Nick," Tammy said.

Blast it, she's not joking!

Then something dawned on me. Tammy was confused that I was asking about Kanae because she thought I was interested in Yoshie! I had never mentioned which sister had caught my eye, and since both sisters are beautiful but only one was not in a relationship, she'd assumed I'd been attracted to Yoshie, who was closer to my age. That's why Tammy hadn't told me earlier about Kanae's boyfriend!

I've heard people talk about having a sinking feeling, but I never knew what they meant until that moment. I felt like the bottom had dropped out of the entire world and I was plunging deep into an abyss.

God, please help me handle this with grace, I prayed.

LOVE NICK-ED

It's scary how often our lives suddenly turn into television sitcoms, isn't it? My parents probably could have written a hit series, *I Love Nicky,* for all the crazy episodes I've acted out over the years. This was a classic!

I wasn't laughing at the time, of course. There is a line in *The Butterfly Circus,* the award-winning short film in which I appeared: "The greater the struggle, the more glorious the triumph." This seems to be true in many aspects of life and even sometimes in relationships.

If love comes easily for you, be grateful and give thanks. If you have to struggle to find your soul mate, as I certainly did, know that in my case the eventual triumph was indeed glorious. Believe in that, and I will pray that it comes true for you as it did for me. I have so much gratitude and appreciation for the way my life has turned out. I can't even say anymore that my ridiculously good life has come about *despite* my disabilities and the hardships I've faced. Now, I must say that my grand life is *because* of my disabilities and hardships.

Does that make sense to you? Here's what I mean: the victories in my life have a richness and depth of meaning for me that I can't imagine would exist if I had been born with arms and legs. I honestly appreciate my life more because I've had to struggle to do many things that most people simply take for granted.

Have there been times when I prayed for arms and legs and fewer obstacles in my path? Certainly. I still pray for those blessings from time to time. I'm not any different than most. I'd much rather take the easy road than the rough one. Yet I also thank God every day for all the good that has come of the disabilities and challenges He's given me.

I encourage you to see your own challenges in relationships and other aspects of your life as potential blessings that one day will come to you, even though their value may not yet be apparent. Sitting there on Tammy's couch, I certainly did not see the value in the fact that the young woman I'd been obsessing over was not available. When I learned that Kanae had a boyfriend, I thought my heart might burst inside my chest.

She looked at me with such warmth and interest, how could she have a boyfriend? Was I kidding myself? Am I deranged?

Just then, Kanae entered with her boyfriend, who dashed up the stairs as soon as he came in the door and did not see me.

Tammy did. Watching from the kitchen, she noted my look of disappointment, and her face went white. She realized where my heart had been directed when I struggled to smile at Kanae's enthusiastic hug. Actually, I've never been so cold and mean to a girl in my life. Playing it cool was no longer in the game plan.

"So, you have a boyfriend?" I said. "How long have you been going out together?"

"About a year," said Kanae.

The abyss suddenly seemed deeper.

I was so mad at myself for misreading this girl who obviously had no interest in me beyond friendship. I wanted to go off somewhere and use my forehead to pound nails, but there was steaming homemade lasagna on the table. Dinner was being served. Kanae's boyfriend joined us, introducing himself. He was friendly and seemed like a nice enough bloke, but I wasn't much in the mood to buddy up. God forgive me, this guy hadn't done a thing to me other than have a girlfriend whom I'd fallen for like a sad sack of bricks.

I managed to get through the meal without biting off the head of the poor unsuspecting boyfriend. My caregiver and I were staying at Tammy's house and so were Kanae and Yoshie, so this was looking like a long night.

I wonder if there's a Red Roof Inn nearby? I thought.

But that would have been bad manners and hard to explain. I had to buck up and make the best of a bad situation. I joined Tammy and her kids in the recreation room, burrowing into a comfy spot on the couch. Kanae joined us after her boyfriend left. When Tammy and the kids went off to bed, I was left alone with my crush, and I briefly thought about pouring out my heart to her. I decided instead to maintain some dignity and let it go.

Maybe I sighed a couple of times. I might even have whimpered once or twice. Despite great temptation I did not cry like a banshee. I was so busy wallowing in self-pity that I did not see Kanae leave her chair. Suddenly, she plopped down on the couch next to me and stared intently into my eyes.

You are so beautiful, and you have no idea how I feel about you, I thought.

"Nick, can I talk to you about something?" she asked.

My Ice Man act melted. I could not resist this woman. I could barely breathe around her. Using every ounce of what little self-control I still had, I responded as matter-of-factly as a quivering, lovesick mass of a man possibly could. I was thankful my nearby caregiver was listening to some music with his eyes shut.

"Sure, what's up?"

The woman of my dreams proceeded to pour out her heart to me—about her boyfriend. The relationship wasn't what she'd hoped it would be. Kanae had doubts and concerns about where it was headed. Her family did not approve of him, and she had been pondering a breakup for several months, even before we met. She liked him, but he was not the one she wanted to spend the rest of her life with, she explained.

I put on my best "listening intently" expression. My concerned and caring face. My wise and empathetic look.

As much as I wanted to be the crowbar that pried Kanae apart from her boyfriend, I knew she was seeking my guidance and putting her trust in me. Like a judge who has a conflict of interest, I had to remove myself from this case and defer to the most Supreme Court.

"I understand your concerns. They are valid. You should pray and ask God to help you make a decision," I said.

If she had simply thanked me for my advice, left me on the couch, and walked away, our story may well have ended there. Instead, she lingered, so close, with those big, warm, dark eyes.

I heard the words and at first couldn't believe they were coming from my mouth: "I have a question for you. Would you tell me what comes to your mind when I say two words: Bell Tower?"

"Our eyes," she replied without hesitation.

"What do you mean?" I asked.

"Our eyes," she said again. "I felt something when we looked at each other, and I freaked out because I've never felt that with anyone before."

Whoa! It wasn't just me, after all, I thought.

"Nick, ever since then I've been praying and fasting on what to do," Kanae said.

"Why didn't you tell me you had a boyfriend back then at the Bell Tower?"

"I was going to ask Tammy for your e-mail to tell you everything, but then Tammy told me that you texted her about my sister taking your breath away..."

"No, no, no," I said. "That text to Tammy was about you, not Yoshie."

"It was about me?"

"You were the one I talked the most to that day. You were the one who caught my eye and held it during my speech, and you were the one I texted about to Tammy."

"Well, I thought you were just a player flirting with us both!"

"No," I insisted.

We both paused a second.

"So, now, you are telling me that you were praying to God and fasting about me?" I asked.

"Yes, I didn't know what to do," Kanae said. "I have a boyfriend, but I'd never felt what I felt when you looked at me."

"Are you serious?" I said.

She fell silent.

Me too.

We'd run out of words. We'd been drawn to each other, but we'd both been torturing ourselves because of a misunderstanding. Our eyes locked again, and the longer we sat there, the more I never wanted to look anywhere else.

I was mesmerized.

Then panicked.

I felt an overwhelming urge to lean forward and kiss her. The emotional barriers were down. We'd opened up and shared our hearts. Yet she still had a boyfriend, which saddened me beyond belief.

She sensed what I was thinking.

"What do we do?" she asked.

"We can't do anything. We've got to let this go. You have a boyfriend."

Did I really just say that? I thought.

"You'd better go now," I told her. *Because I want to kiss you so badly,* I thought.

I was whipsawed by thoughts of joy and feelings of panic. This beautiful young woman had genuine feelings for me. She could love me! But she still had a boyfriend.

I had to put my feelings on lockdown.

"Give me a hug and go upstairs now," I told her. "We need to pray for God's help. No matter what these feelings are, we need to ask God to take them away."

I was torn, and so was Kanae. We decided to go our separate ways and believe by faith that if we were meant to be together, God would do miracles.

After Kanae left, I prayed on the couch for at least an hour, asking God first to calm my heart. Then I prayed for Him to help me stop wanting to be with Kanae if He did not want us to be together. I tried to convince myself that if she was not the one, I could just move on.

I dreamed of Kanae all night, and then in the morning, I had to say goodbye to her. Before leaving, she and Tammy and I huddled in the kitchen and talked through all that had happened. Tammy apologized for assuming that I'd been referring to Yoshie instead of Kanae when I texted about my feelings after the Bell Tower speech. We accepted her apology and forgave her for an honest mistake. Then we said our farewells to one another.

I left, not knowing if I'd ever see Kanae again, let alone be with her one day. I was emotionally exhausted from the highs and lows of the last twenty-four hours. All I could do was put it in God's hands, but that didn't stop my heart from aching. There was some consolation in the fact that she had admitted to having feelings for me. Just knowing that meant a lot to me. Her attraction to me confirmed that I wasn't making up things in my head or thinking wishfully.

The fact that a smart, godly, and beautiful young woman like Kanae could see me as someone she might love was itself a blessing, and I had to acknowledge and thank God for this great gift. Kanae had impressed me as a Proverbs 31 woman, a wife or woman of noble character. Her character and faith in God blew me away. Part of putting faith into action in relationships is working to be your best and then believing that it is possible for someone to love you. It's about believing there is a person out there who could look at you, see beyond all your flaws and shortcomings, and still love you.

My story should encourage you in this. Know that if it is possible for me, it is possible for you. If that is not enough, look around you. The world is full of imperfect, normal people who have found love and companionship. Love is possible for you too. I pray that your soul mate finds you soon, and I pray also that your bonds are stronger than the challenges you will face.

WORKING IT OUT

Six weeks passed without any communication from Kanae. I had to return to Dallas for another engagement, and I was torn about whether I should call her. Tammy had extended a standing invitation for me to stay at her house whenever I was in the area, but I didn't want to put Kanae in an awkward position. I decided to stay with another friend in town, but I forgot to call him to check if he'd be around. When I called him from the Dallas airport, he was out of town.

My caregiver and I had been traveling so much neither of us wanted to stay another night in a hotel. I was road weary and feeling down. My mind, body, and soul were weak, and so was my willpower. The thought of seeing Kanae and maybe talking to her a little bit—even if her boyfriend were still in the picture—trumped any thought of staying in a hotel.

I called Tammy to see if we could spend the night. Mark and the kids were home and welcomed us to come by, so we headed their way. And, yes, Kanae was there too.

During the drive from the airport, I had another talk with God.

You know I'm tired, and I am going to Tammy's instead of a hotel. You know who is there and... I smiled at God's sense of humor. I suspected God was smiling too.

I should have been more apprehensive and guarded, but I was so exhausted and disoriented from my travels that I had a goofy grin on my face. "This is going to be fun," I told my friend as we pulled into the driveway.

Mark and Tammy's kids ran out, greeted us, and grabbed our bags, so we went into the kitchen. Kanae was there and we locked eyes.

"Surprise!" I said, feeling a little sheepish.

She laughed and smiled. If I'd had legs, I'm sure they would have gone weak. As it was, I felt as though I'd walked out of a one-dimensional, black-and-white world into a 3-D Technicolor planet. The chemistry between us was ten times stronger than before, and any remaining doubts were dissipated as soon as Kanae walked up, placed a hand on my shoulder, and said, "After praying all this time, God has put peace in my heart to break up with my boyfriend. I want to be with someone who I can see spending the rest of my life with."

Yes!

All the disappointments, struggles, failures, fears, and tears in my life became irrelevant and forgotten in that God-given moment of victory. My mind could hardly wrap around the fact that such a special young woman was saying that she would be willing to spend the rest of her life as my wife.

My wife!

Kanae told me that she'd been attracted to me from our first meeting, but beyond that, she'd felt such a strong emotional connection that it scared her. Mature beyond her years, she wanted to act on faith, not emotion, so after we first met, she pulled back and prayed for God's guidance.

"I prayed for God to tell me what those feelings were, whether they were just a physical chemistry or emotions, or if this really was God's call for a lasting relationship," she said. "I didn't want to rely on my emotions. I didn't want to step forward only for that reason, so I just kept praying." In other words, Kanae put her faith into action.

My prayer for you is that someday, when you are ready to receive it,

God will put contentment in your heart, either by blessing you with someone who loves you or by allowing you to feel fully blessed without someone. Prepare yourself by staying in faith and being the best person you can be. Give as much love as you can. Put it out there, and God will take care of the rest.

Love Tested

As much as that moment felt like the greatest romantic movie ever written—or at least the greatest in which I had a starring role—it was not a movie. This was real life, and you know how that can go. Once we committed to each other without reservations, the next step was to introduce ourselves as a couple to our families.

Kanae's mother and sister gave their blessings right away, and I was very grateful for their love and understanding. When she told her mum, my future mother-in-law actually said, "Glory to God!"

Yoshie had told her mum weeks earlier that there was chemistry between Kanae and me, and their mum said she had been praying and fasting that a relationship would blossom. I won over her grandmother, aunts, uncles, and cousins by dancing to a mariachi band at a family party and then sharing my faith with them. They weren't worried about my lack of limbs. A few harbored concerns that I might be a shallow celebrity who lacked substance, but after I shared my testimony and Kanae and I professed our love for each other, those fears went away.

I actually put off telling my parents about this new relationship for a couple of weeks because my dad tends to be wary and likes to interrogate me when it comes to women. My mum and dad quickly came to love Kanae too. She has a level of wisdom rare for such a young lady. Her parents divorced when she was five years old, and Kanae had to take on some adult responsibilities at that early age.

Her maturity became especially apparent when my parents asked Kanae a very difficult question. While my lack of limbs was not the result of an inherited gene—my brother and sister have all their limbs—my parents nonetheless asked how she would feel if one of our children came into the world like me.

My future bride, who had already decided she wanted a large family, replied, "Even if all five of our kids have no arms and no legs, I would love them all. And I know I have it easier than you, because Nick came out of the blue for you, but I would have him as their role model and guide."

Kanae told my parents that she loved me, and she would love our children too. In the past I had worried that I'd never find a woman whom my parents would approve of because they are so protective of me. But God brought me a young woman who won their respect, their admiration, and their hearts.

Her feelings for me were obviously very sincere, and she expressed them with a depth that fills me with awe, humility, and gratitude. But it's not just what she says that makes me appreciate and love her so much, she expresses her love for me with actions and deeds each and every day.

I first observed the depth of her caring for me in December 2010. We were only a few months into our relationship when I learned of the cash-flow problems at my business. We were not yet engaged, but marriage was definitely on the table. This was a time when I wanted my potential future bride to see me in the best possible light. Instead, she saw me at my darkest. Maybe, just maybe, there is a worse time in a new relationship to have a total meltdown, but I can't think of one. There we were, a couple very much in the early stages, and the allegedly strong male went over a cliff and into a valley of despair.

In the previous chapter I gave you all the sorry details of my highly emotional overreaction to a temporary cash-flow problem at Attitude Is Altitude during the economic recession. What I did not tell you is that during the meltdown Kanae proved that her love for me is boundless.

I have never felt the power of unconditional love at such strength. Now that is saying something, because my parents, my brother and my sister, and all my aunts, uncles, and cousins have shown me nothing but unconditional love all my life. Yet they are family. Blood ties are one thing. Kanae's ties to me were far more tenuous and newly formed. She very easily could have walked away. Instead, she came closer. She put her faith and her love into action in ways that seemed heroic to me.

At a time when I wanted to present myself as a successful provider, I had to admit to my new girlfriend that my business had fallen fifty thousand dollars in debt. In my anxiety I felt like a penniless failure. Why she didn't run out the door and never look back, I don't know, but I will be forever grateful that she chose instead to remain by my side, soothing me and encouraging me with her love.

I put a value on my worth as a human being when I felt worthless because of my business debt. Kanae reminded me that love doesn't look for price tags. She demonstrated in words and actions that her interest was not in measuring what I had to give. Instead, she poured out for me all the caring, nurturing, and sustaining love she possessed.

One of the thoughts that really bothered me about the debt was that I'd been hoping to put some money into savings so I could pull back on my speaking schedule for a year or so. I didn't want to be traveling all the time during our first year of marriage. Family and friends had been telling me for years that I should slow down, and finally I had a good reason to do just that—my wife-to-be.

When I told Kanae that my for-profit business was profitless and in debt, her response was, "That doesn't matter to me. I'll get a nursing job and support the both of us."

She did not hesitate. She did not flinch. She did not run for the door. She ran her fingers through my hair, comforted me, and let me know she would always be there for me.

It meant so much to me also that I knew Kanae was praying for me every day. Emotional support can be a big blessing, but prayers are even more powerful. To know that she understood my needs and prayed that they would be filled was so comforting. God is the ultimate provider of peace and patience, and Kanae prayed for Him to heal me and give me peace and joy.

I realized that she had become the bridge to all that I can be in Christ. Kanae is the key to my becoming all that I can be as a husband, speaker, evangelist, friend, boss, brother, and son. With her, I don't have to ask for anything. I don't have to tell her what I need. She knows. She feels what I feel, and she encourages me, but more important, she stands in the gap with prayer and asks God to give me what she can't provide, which is His wisdom, His healing, His peace, and His patience. Finally, Kanae gives me her empathy. She is my greatest empathizer. Everything that affects me affects her. She is there for me, and I always want to be there for her when she needs to talk and to vent.

You know you are in a loving relationship when you are willing to give without receiving anything in return, when you put the other person's needs above your own. I put Kanae above my ministry and my businesses, which means spending time together, watching movies, sitting in front of the fire, and just talking through our lives. I'm increasingly amazed at how many layers there are to a relationship like ours. The more Kanae gives to me, the more I want to be worthy of her love and devotion. She makes me want to be better.

A friend was telling me one day about his new relationship, and he kept saying, "I think she is too good for me. I don't deserve this woman." I told him that was a great place for him to be at that point in his relationship. We should be with people who inspire us and motivate us to grow, to be more godly, more caring, more giving, more empathetic. I am already a much more patient man than ever before. Of course the bar was not set real high during my single days when I tended to be self-centered and impatient.

My uncle Batta recently reminded me of a journal I kept years ago, and in it I'd made a list of ten things I wanted in my wife.

"Does Kanae fulfill all the things on the list?" he asked.

I had to go back and check it. Then I called him and said, "As a matter of fact, yes! Every one of them!"

It was a funny moment, and beautiful too.

I may be a few years older than Kanae, but she is wise in ways I've yet to learn. She has established the foundation for a relationship that is not contaminated by expectations or distractions or subconscious hopes. I believe this is a love that will grow deeper and richer over time. I've often said that if you aren't growing in faith, then you are shrinking in it, and so it is with love. She is truly a child of God. She is royalty, and God has given her to me so that we can love each other and honor Him for His blessings.

Our love is contagious. An elderly woman saw us together one day, talking and laughing, and she came up to us with tears in her eyes and said, "Now I believe in true love again." I can't explain to you the joy I have when I see Kanae smiling or laughing, dancing, singing, and having fun. I can't wait for the day when we can watch our children do the same.

You are God's creation and therefore worthy of His love, which makes you worthy of a loving relationship too. I pray that you are as blessed by love as I have been, but remember to do your part and prepare yourself to not only receive it but to give it unselfishly too.

FOUR

A Life of Passion and Purpose

EARLY IN MY LIFE, WHEN MY PARENTS WERE TRYING TO LOOK AHEAD AND figure out what sort of future I might have, my father, the accountant, suggested that I follow him into his profession. "You are good with numbers, and you can always hire other people to be your arms and legs," my dad said.

Crunching numbers is fun for me. Counting on my fingers and toes is not an option, but thanks to modern technology and my little foot, I can use a calculator and computer easily enough. So in college I went along with the parental plan and majored in financial planning and accounting. The thought of helping people make good monetary decisions, creating wealth for them and mapping out strategic plans for sustenance, appealed to me. I also enjoyed trading in the stock market, where I had both good and bad experiences.

Working as a financial planner seemed like a good way to serve others while supporting myself and, I hoped, my family too. Still, I never felt fully committed to that plan. There was always the sense that God was calling me to follow a different path. I'd begun giving talks about my disabilities to classmates in junior high. They responded to my words. I touched something in them, and God lit the sparks of a passion He'd placed within me.

Over time I spoke more and more about my faith. Evangelism and inspiration became my greatest passions. Speaking about my love of God and the blessings in my life, including my disabilities and the strength they give me, allows me to serve others. It's given my life a purpose, one that I believe God created for me.

That is a great gift. Many people struggle to find meaning and direction in their lives. They question their value because they aren't clear on how they can contribute or make a mark. Maybe you haven't identified where your talents and interests lie. It's not uncommon to cast about trying one thing or another before identifying your life's calling. Changing course several times is increasingly common.

I encourage you to identify whatever it is that fulfills you and engages all your gifts and energy. Pursue that path, not for your own glory or enrichment, but to honor God and to make a contribution. Be patient if it takes time to find your way. Know that timing is important and that as long as you hold a true passion in your heart, it will not fade. Understand that even passions can come with risk. Remember, too, that if one passion ends, it is probably because God has something bigger and better in mind for you.

FINDING YOUR PASSION

You'll know you've found a passion when your talents, knowledge, energy, focus, and commitment all come together in a way that excites you like a child with a favorite game or toy. Your work and pleasure become one and the same. You feel as though the opportunities are endless. What you do becomes part of who you are, and the rewards that come to you are far less satisfying than those that come to others because of you.

Your passion leads you to your purpose, and both are activated when you put your faith in your gifts and share them with the world. You are custom-made for your purpose, just as I am for mine. Every part of you—from your mental, physical, and spiritual strengths to your unique package of talents and experiences—is designed to fulfill that gift.

You put your faith in action by following your passion, defining your purpose, and building your life around developing and using your gifts to their fullest. What drives you? What makes you excited about each day? What would you do for free just to be doing it? What would you never want to retire from doing? Is there something that you would give up everything else for—all your material possessions and comforts—just to do because you feel so good doing it? What do you feel a sense of urgency about accomplishing?

Scripture tells us in John 9:4, "As long as it is day, we must do the works of him who sent me. Night is coming, when no one can work." If you haven't found the work God intends for you, ask yourself the questions from the previous paragraph. If that doesn't help you identify a passion, try asking those closest to you for their assessments and suggestions. What talents have they identified in you? Where do they think you could make a mark or a difference? What do they see you being most enthusiastic about?

Finally, before you decide what your passion is, I strongly suggest you check with the Ultimate Authority on the subject. I'm often asked how we can tell what God wants us to do. Whether you are trying to decide what your passion is, or you are facing a difficult situation and uncertain of what to do, my advice is to pursue God's love and get to know Him as a friend so that you can enjoy His presence. Pray to Him and meditate on His Word.

To know and believe in God is the best thing that can happen in your life because He can turn what appears to be the worst event into the best. He can transform your struggles into your learning. He can turn your suffering into strength. He can use your failures to bring success.

God has the power to give you "beauty for ashes, the oil of joy for mourning [and] the garment of praise for the spirit of heaviness." If you are puzzled as to what His plan is for you and uncertain of which passion to pursue, pray to God for guidance. Ask others to pray for you as well. If the answer doesn't come to you, my suggestion is that you find a way to serve others, whether on a mission trip or in your community. Try that for a while to see what comes of it.

I assure you, God pays for what He orders. He would not call you into His service without providing all you need to pursue your passion and purpose. At first you may not understand your calling. You may think that you lack passion for it. My dad was called to start a church, which he had no interest in doing. Yet he honored God and did what he felt called to do. Dad struggled at first with this. I'm sure Noah, too, had doubts when God put in an order for an enormous ark, but he didn't say a word. He just built the boat. Following that order turned out to be a wise move. My father, like Noah, was eventually very grateful that he complied with his calling to build a church. People were drawn to it, and his work as a lay minister changed lives.

When God calls you to do something, you may not understand or be enthusiastic at first. But you should always be passionate about Him, which means you will do anything for Him. I've been blessed in that way. My calling is to speak and inspire. My passion is to connect my listeners with God and with the best that is within them.

TIMING IS CRITICAL

The timing was right for me to become a public speaker because, at that point, I did not have a family to support or any major financial commitments. I'd spent years speaking for free, but fortunately there were people willing to pay to hear me speak. Those fees allowed me to support myself but also covered my speaking expenses for those I wanted to reach who could not afford to pay me.

Sometimes, though, we may be tempted to rush into the things we are passionate about without considering whether the timing is right. Exhibit A: *Me!*

My company's debt problems in 2010 were partly the result of cost overruns incurred in the production of a Christian music video I wanted to do out of my passion for singing, but I did not adequately consider whether the timing was right. The song I performed on the video is "Something More," which proved to be ironic, since the production costs turned out to be something more than I'd budgeted for—a lot more. I rushed to make my music video, and in my enthusiasm for the project, I let the costs get out of control. I wanted to make a dream into a reality. Someone should have reminded me that dreams don't die as long as you hold them dear.

That's not to say the music video wasn't a great experience. We had a talented team of people, including singer and songwriter Tyrone Wells as well as Matthew Koppin, who led the video production team. We created a movie-quality Christian music video, thanks also to Jon and Esther

Phelps, whose support made it possible to have the first-class song track recorded in their studio with an awesome team of band members flown in from Nashville. I consider the video a success because it reached 1.6 million people on YouTube with a message of hope.

I also learned a valuable lesson. Timing is an important consideration in any endeavor, especially for someone building a business and a brand for the long term. I had just branched out into acting, with the award-winning short film *The Butterfly Circus*. Cranking out a music video so soon after that may have left many people wondering, *What's Nick up to now? Is he still an evangelist and inspirational speaker, or is he an actor and singer?*

One day I hope to be all those things on some level, but there is no rush. I am still in my twenties. I have a few good years left. Impatience is another characteristic of youth, of course. Since the age of sixteen, I've been in a rush to prove myself in so many arenas that I've often run my poor body ragged, and I've sometimes stretched my resources to the breaking point. The financial setbacks with my business served to remind me that I don't have to do everything all at once.

A friend wrote a humorous book of advice for high school and college graduates, and one of his tidbits is "Hurry up and learn patience." There is wisdom as well as a little humor in that. The Bible often extols the virtues of patience. In James 5 we're told, "Be patient, then, brothers and sisters, until the Lord's coming. See how the farmer waits for the land to yield its valuable crop, patiently waiting for the autumn and spring rains. You too, be patient and stand firm, because the Lord's coming is near."

Just because you have the resources today doesn't mean the timing is right. No doubt, ambition and energy have led to the creation of many great businesses and careers, but timing is critical. That's why patience is a virtue and taking a leap is a risk. I'm not opposed to risk; in fact, I pride myself on taking well-calculated risks in which I do everything possible to reduce any potential downside. In the case of the music video, however, I didn't do enough analysis of all the factors. Remember to consider *all* the risks involved. Do your best to minimize them as you pursue your passion.

PASSION OF BIBLICAL PROPORTIONS

Risks often bring rewards, but, as in the case of Caleb, you may have to be patient in awaiting their arrival. Caleb is one of the Bible's best examples of a truly passionate man who took considerable risks while putting his faith into action. After Moses and the twelve tribes fled Egypt to escape slavery, Moses sent twelve spies into Canaan, the land God had promised them. Ten of the spies reported that the land would be impossible to claim because the inhabitants, whom they described as "giants," would be impossible to defeat. Only two spies, Caleb and Joshua, said that the people could take the land with God's help. But Moses chose the advice of the ten over the two. They did not try to take the Promised Land, and some threatened to stone the two spies who had wanted to follow God's orders.

The Hebrews were then forced to wander in the desert for forty years as punishment for disobeying God's order to take the land as theirs. Of the twelve spies, only the two who asserted that the people should take the land survived those forty years of wandering. God even hailed Caleb as "my servant," a term of honor previously used only for Moses.

By the time the Hebrews finally occupied the Promised Land, Caleb was in his eighties, but he was still strong and passionate about his faith. After the victory, God gave Caleb and his descendants the city of Hebron and its outskirts as a reward for following God "wholeheartedly" and for putting his faith into action once again. As the hymn says, "to patient faith the prize is sure," and Caleb was rewarded for being a man who never lost his passion for serving God.

Caleb paid a steep price for remaining dedicated. His own people threatened to kill him, and then he was left wandering in the desert with them for four decades before finally leading them to victory. Pursuing your passion will likely bring many rewards, but that does not mean your life will be free of challenges or struggles.

Any dedicated person, whether a nurse, artist, builder, pastor, or performer, can tell you that hard work, sacrifice, and enormous effort are required, even of those who love what they do. I have spent most of the last ten years on airplanes and in hotel rooms around the world in my mission to speak encouragement and faith to as many people as I can. Although I am probably the only frequent flyer who has never complained about legroom on an airplane, constant travel is as exhausting for me as anyone. I have reached millions of people, and I've seen many of them renew their faith or become born again, and I am grateful beyond measure for those experiences. Yet pursuing my passion has not been easy. I've had to make sacrifices. With God's help and the support and prayers of those who encourage me in my ministry, I've had some wonderful successes. By God's grace I will be able to build upon them.

Most passion-driven people sacrifice and struggle. Helen Keller overcame deafness and blindness to become an inspiration to people around the world. She said, "Character cannot be developed in ease and quiet. Only through experience of trial and suffering can the soul be strengthened, ambition inspired, and success achieved."

"Overnight success" is usually the result of many years of hard work. Resting on your laurels is rarely an option. Yet there is probably no greater reward than doing what you were created to do while serving a purpose greater than yourself. I meet so many men and women in my travels who are on a mission to make a difference by sharing their gifts and knowledge. We share war stories of the road, and we support and encourage one another.

CALLED FOR A PURPOSE

One of my most passionate fellow travelers on the evangelical road is Victor Marx, whose story is remarkable. Victor served in the US Marine Corps, and he is a martial arts expert who holds a seventh-degree black belt in Keichu-Do self-defense, which incorporates elements of karate; judo, ju-jitsu, kung fu, and street-fighting techniques.

He has trained more than thirty world champions in martial arts as well as Navy SEALs, Army Rangers, and Delta Force. His wife, Eileen, is a former Miss Fitness USA, and as you might imagine, Victor is in great physical shape too. Looking at him, you would be shocked to know that he once considered himself to be damaged goods. He told me that he and I have much in common except that my disability challenges are quite visible while his are hidden from sight, locked inside his mind and spirit.

People often say they don't know how I've created such a meaningful and fulfilling life despite my lack of limbs. Yet I am blessed in more ways than I can count. I think life would be far more difficult for someone who lacks a loving family like the one I had. Sadly, Victor grew up in a broken home, and it is no wonder that he once felt broken himself.

Victor became a Christian while in the service. Ten years ago he was operating a successful chain of martial arts academies in Hawaii while also doing Christian outreach to young people. He was enjoying a very good life with Eileen and their three children when God called. Focus on the

Family, the Colorado-based organization that promotes Christian values, called to recruit him for a leadership position.

No one in his family wanted to leave Hawaii, but Victor and Eileen acted in faith, choosing to trust and obey. Victor did not have a passion to give up his business and join Focus on the Family. He could not understand what God had in mind for him, but like Noah, he yielded to the calling put upon him.

You see, God knew something about Victor that he did not know about himself.

My friend had long suffered from nightmares and anxiety. He attributed some of them to his days in the marines and even to his martial arts combat. He also had flashbacks of violent incidents that he could not fully comprehend, because they did not seem related to the military or martial arts. Some of those flashbacks were revealed during a small-group Bible study that Victor and Eileen participated in with other top staff members from Focus on the Family and their spouses. The study provided a safe environment for them to talk candidly about their lives and feelings.

"We were asked to share our life stories, which was something I'd never done before publicly," Victor told me. "I always had trust issues."

Victor attributed his lack of trust to his troubled upbringing in the Deep South. Initially, he shared only the condensed and cleaned-up version of his story with his coworkers that night. He told them his parents had divorced before he was even born. As a child, he never knew his father, who had a history of dealing drugs and promoting prostitution. Growing up, Victor had thought his first stepfather was his real father. Then his mother divorced and married six times. He and his siblings were raised in dysfunction and chaos. Because of his mother's tumultuous life, Victor attended fourteen schools and lived in seventeen houses by the time he graduated from high school.

When Victor finished giving that brief version of his life, a friend said, "Now we'd like to hear the rest of your story."

Victor was puzzled by this and unnerved.

"They all were looking at me like I was under suspicion for something," he recalled.

When he asked what was meant by "the rest of your story," his friend said, "You can't have these sorts of things happen in your life without there being more to your story."

Victor knew these people cared about him. As they probed gently into his life, "The truth came pouring out of me—things that I'd held inside and never told anyone, not even my wife."

That night marked the beginning of a long period of revelation, reconciliation, and healing for Victor. "It took several years to peel the onion and to come to terms with all that had happened to me," he said.

Victor had suppressed horrific memories from his childhood, including what he calls the "nonprovables"—meaning abuse to which there were no witnesses—that tend to torment the victims of abuse. One stepfather tortured him, held his head underwater, and put a gun to his head. He had been sexually and physically abused between the ages of three and seven. Once he was molested and left for dead in a locked commercial cooler. He escaped only because family members "found me and thawed me out."

Victor had suffered unspeakable cruelties. Like most victims of abuse, he harbored deep psychological and emotional hurt as well as intense anger. Much of it he had locked away, which was a credit to the strength of his will. Amazingly, he had succeeded in channeling his anger and violent urges into positive ways through his military career and martial arts training and competitions.

Still, so much had been inflicted upon him that Victor could not manage all the pain. He sought counseling, and his doctors told him that his flashbacks, as well as some involuntary physical ticks and a mild form of trauma-based Tourette's syndrome, were related to his posttraumatic stress disorder, which is common in victims of childhood abuse. One psychiatrist told him that his brain had been scrambled by the horrors he had endured, so his mind did not process thoughts in a normal manner and never would.

Along with professional treatment for PTSD, Victor's powerful faith helped him learn to deal with the revived memories and the trauma they triggered. Over time he shared the story of his childhood and his walk of faith. He found an especially receptive audience in troubled young men and women, including juvenile offenders, gang members, youth prison inmates, foster-care kids, and residents of drug treatment centers. He learned to first capture their interest with martial arts demonstrations and self-deprecating humor, telling them, "I'm a cross between Jackie Chan and Barney Fife."

Most of the young people Victor speaks to have little patience for adult speakers offering life lessons, but he discovered that his story resonates with troubled young men and women because many of them have suffered physical and sexual abuse as children too.

"I had lived with so much denial, I didn't realize I even had a story, and I wasn't sure I should be telling it," he said. "One day in the early going, I was doing a nun-chucks demonstration for a group of juvenile offenders, and I accidentally hit one of my volunteers in the chin and split it open! I thought God was trying to tell me to stop, and I was worried about ending up in jail for assault, but that day, fifty-three of the seventy-five inmates in that prison gave their lives to Christ."

To Victor's surprise, many churches also requested that he speak to their congregations to share his story of redemption. His story offers testimony to the power of faith in action through his victory over a tragic childhood and his pursuit of a passion to serve troubled young people.

Now, Victor understands why God called him to leave a comfortable life in Hawaii. There are very few people who can reach at-risk youths and violent offenders like Victor can, in part because a high percentage of them have also been emotionally, physically, and sexually abused. When a man like Victor speaks openly of his pain, he brings others to healing.

"God supernaturally has given me a heart for these people. I understand what is behind their pain," he said. "I encourage them to get help by giving them permission to open up and seek counseling."

Once he began sharing his story publicly, Victor could not keep up with the requests for speaking engagements. To his great surprise, unsolicited donations also began arriving in the mail. In 2003 he and his wife formed a nonprofit evangelistic organization, All Things Possible, and two years later they received a surprise $250,000 donation from a couple who'd heard of their work and wanted to support it.

"We were worried that we'd never be able to support ourselves doing this type of work, but we've seen unbelievable things happen since we committed to it and put our faith in God," Victor said. "We think God loves these kids who are locked up and hurting. There are few folks reaching them on a national scale, so we plan to keep doing this until God says I'm done."

CHANGING COURSE

While both Victor and I were led to become evangelists, there are many ways to make a contribution while pursuing your passion. Your unique package of talents, education, and experience may be suited for business, public service, the arts, or other fields. The important thing is to recognize what God has put in you and to build your life around those gifts and passions by taking action even when you may not fully understand what drives them or where they will lead you.

I abandoned plans for a career in accounting to pursue my passion for speaking. Victor gave up a comfortable and secure life as the owner of a successful martial arts academy to follow God's plan. You, too, may one day come to a life-changing fork in the road. It is never too late for that to happen.

The Bible offers us the story of Saul, a noted persecutor of Christians, who was blinded by a bright light while on the road to Damascus. Jesus then spoke to him and directed him to proceed into the city where he would learn of his new path in life. After three days, God restored his sight. He was then baptized and given the name Paul. He became a major Christian evangelist, driven by a passion for spreading the good news of the death and resurrection of Jesus Christ. God showed him his purpose, and Paul acted upon his faith, pursuing it passionately for the rest of his life. You can make a mark in this world by doing the same thing. Believe it, and know that it is always possible to change the course of your life for the better. Paul's transformation from a persecutor of Christians to leading evangelist was deemed a miracle. I believe that such dramatic transformations are possible for any of us.

My message for you is that no matter where you are right now in life, you should never think all is lost. You may have strayed from the righteous course. You may even have done terrible things, but that does not mean you cannot turn your life around, find a new passion, and become a force for good in this world.

I didn't mention this earlier, but the person who led Victor Marx to Jesus Christ was his birth father, Karl. Yes, the man who had abandoned him before Victor was born, who had been a drug dealer and pimp, turned his life around and then reached out and brought his son to God.

Victor was in the marines when he received a letter from Karl. Previously Karl had denied that Victor was his child, abandoned Victor's mother, and rejected any responsibility for him. Karl first met Victor when his son was six years old, but he still had little contact with him over the years. Then he wrote a letter to Victor. When Victor opened it, he was disgusted that the handwritten letter began "Dear Son," because this man had never been a father to him. Nevertheless, he read on.

His father wrote of his remorse over his decadent life and lack of involvement with Victor. He had been a criminal and even spent time in a mental hospital. This news did not shock Victor, but the next sentence did. "I know you're going to think I'm crazy, but I've gone crazy for Jesus Christ," Karl wrote.

Victor's father had discovered that "our God is a God who brings hope to the hopeless" and that no matter what sort of life you've led, "Somebody loves you just the same. Somebody is waiting patiently for you to find peace for your anxious soul. God's forgiveness and love is powerful enough to cover a world of sin and shame."

In his letter, Karl invited Victor to visit him on his next military leave. Victor agreed. They went to church together, and there Victor felt the love of God more intensely than ever before. He was filled with a passion for bringing others to God, and he has acted upon that passion ever since.

A FORCE FOR GOOD

One of the dangers of modern society is that so many people value what they do or what they own more than they value who they are. We all have to make a living, but too often we lose perspective on what is truly most important to our eternal salvation. Job status, the amount of money earned, possessions accumulated, and notoriety are false gods. I advocate pursuing your passion, but only if that passion uses your gifts to glorify God, not to exalt the self. I've known misguided people who pursue a passion that is all about feeding their egos and building status. Instead of taking joy in expressing the gifts that God gave them as a way to honor Him and be a blessing to others, their focus shifts to accumulating money, status, and power. In the process they neglect their relationships and their spiritual development.

Yet faith in action has changed many lives, often in incredible ways. Your God-given passion can drive and define your purpose. One of my favorite examples is my friend Eduardo Verástegui, whose story just keeps getting better and better.

Eduardo threw himself into the fame-and-fortune vortex at the age of seventeen. He followed that path from humble beginnings in a small Mexican village all the way to Hollywood. I met Eduardo on the movie set where I had my first acting experience. I was making the short film *The Butterfly Circus.* He was a well-known actor on the film, particularly well known in Latin America. He portrayed the benevolent ringmaster who welcomes me into a special circus that celebrates all people and their unique gifts.

When we began filming, I was a little intimidated to meet Eduardo, especially because our first scene together—which was supposed to be the first scene filmed—called for me to spit in his face! I begged the director to postpone that scene until I felt a little more comfortable on the set. He agreed, but delaying that scene may have been a mistake, because the more I came to know Eduardo, the less I wanted to do such a nasty thing to him. He is an inspiring man of faith.

I didn't know his story until we became friends, which proved easier than I'd thought. I was shocked to learn in our first conversation that this well-known actor was a fan of my videos.

FINDING A TRUE PASSION

Eduardo's life had undergone an incredible transformation by the time we met. He'd grown up in a poor village, the son of a sugarcane farmer. His father wanted him to be a lawyer, but Eduardo quit law school after the second semester "because I realized I was not passionate about it," he said.

He'd already had a taste of fame and fortune as a teenager, and Eduardo decided to continue on that path. "I wanted to become an actor, singer, and model, but for all the wrong reasons," he said. "My reasons were selfish. I loved performing, but I was immature. I wanted success, everything that society pitched—the money, fame, and women, and all those things that were supposed to make me happy. I wanted to be somebody."

In the early 1990s he had joined two other guys in a singing group called Kairo. Their Latino "boy band" experienced major success in Latin America, selling records and performing concerts in fifty countries, usually to audiences of screaming girls. Despite their success Eduardo left the band in 1997 to pursue acting. Soon he was a leading man in Mexican television soap operas known as *telenovelas*, performing in five consecutive series.

Then, in 2001, he moved to Miami and signed a recording contract as a solo artist. He'd already released an album when he was chosen to star as Jennifer Lopez's love interest in a steamy music video. That same year, he landed his first major film role in the Latin comedy *Chasing Papi* as a playboy dating three women at the same time. He also was named one of the hottest Hispanic stars in *People* magazine's Spanish edition.

"I was inside a bubble of vanity, ego, and lust, and sooner or later, if you don't wake up, it will kill you mentally and emotionally," he told me.

One day on a flight from Miami to Los Angeles, Eduardo was seated next to the casting manager for 20th Century Fox Studios. After they'd introduced themselves, the executive said that his studio was looking for a Spanish actor with a thick accent for a new film. He invited Eduardo to read for the part, and he won the role.

Eduardo then moved to L.A., where he hired a tutor to improve his English. She did much more than that. She changed his life.

At twenty-eight years old, Eduardo appeared destined for stardom as an actor and singer. Hollywood proclaimed him "the next Antonio Banderas." He hired agents, managers, and lawyers—more than fifteen people—to help guide his career. But he was not at peace. "I was lost and very confused, which translated into an anger that made me difficult to work with," he said.

Eduardo did not feel the happiness he'd expected because he had strayed from God's plan. He thought his passion was to be a performer, but as he matured, Eduardo realized that using his talents to glorify himself was not the path for him. He was not living a godly life, and this inauthentic existence ate at him.

This is what happens when we stray from our true purpose. Our actions do not match up with our values and principles, and so our passion fades. We lose enthusiasm and energy. We feel out of sorts because we are off the path God has chosen for us. You may have felt that way at times or even now. When you have a deep and abiding unhappiness like Eduardo's, it is usually because you are not living as you were meant to live; your gifts are being used for the wrong purpose.

Do not ignore these feelings. Examine them and trace them to the source so you can get back on track. Often in situations when you have strayed from where God wants you to be, He will send someone to put you back on course. In Eduardo's case this person was his English-language instructor. During their sessions she picked up on his unhappiness, helped him trace the source of it, and encouraged him to pray for guidance.

"I still thought of myself as a good Catholic person because I went to Mass on Christmas and Easter," he said. "I gave myself license to do anything I wanted as long as I didn't hurt anyone or steal anything."

In his talks with his English instructor, Eduardo realized that in his misguided quest for fame and fortune, he'd lost his way spiritually. He'd mistaken excitement and hedonistic self-interest for true, God-given passion. He compared himself to a greyhound chasing a fake rabbit on a dog racetrack. If a dog actually catches the rabbit, he bites into metal and hurts himself, so he never chases it again.

"I was chasing a lie," he said. "When I attained what I'd been after, I only felt pain. My English tutor was a wonderful Christian lady who made me examine what was really important to me, what true success would be, and what I'd been doing with my talents."

He had bought into the macho attitude that "the more women I was with, the better man I was." But when his English instructor asked him if he was the sort of man that a mother would want her daughter to marry, "I realized how stupid I'd been."

She helped Eduardo see that he wasn't just living a macho stereotype, he'd also allowed himself to be cast in roles that only fed the negative stereotypes of Latino men as either Latin lovers obsessed with sex or cut-throat drug dealers and violent thieves.

"My instructor said that I had become part of the problem instead of glorifying God with my talents by promoting family values and positive images," he said. "She blew me away. It broke my heart that I was not using what God had given me to make a positive contribution. What I had been doing reflected badly on my faith and on the Latino culture."

Eduardo went through a period of remorse over the life he'd been leading. He went to confession for the first time in years, promising God that he would begin putting faith into action by living it. He vowed to honor God and his heritage in all that he did. This included honoring women and their dignity.

"I realized that a real man identifies with the life of Jesus Christ and is therefore respectful of women," he said. "I recognize now that sex is a gift from God. It is sacred, and that gift is to be protected and shared with the most important person in my life—apart from God—and that is going to be the mother of my children, if that is my vocation. I discovered the value of chastity, and I made a promise to God that I would never again be with a woman until I marry."

LOOKING WITHIN

Eduardo's reawakening was triggered also by comments from his mother. She told him that she'd said to his father one day, "I don't know what to do with our son. I am afraid he will end up in jail, in the hospital, or dead. Nothing good can come of his lifestyle."

In his desire to change his life, Eduardo walked away from an acting career that was just taking off. He fired his entire team and declined all roles offered him for the next four years. No longer was he interested in being a celebrity. Instead, his passion became to know, love, and serve God. He vowed to never again use his talents except for those purposes.

"If that meant the end of my acting career, then so be it," he said.

In the weeks and months that followed, Eduardo's income plummeted, but he saw that as necessary to his renewal. He attempted to clear out all material distractions so he could once again hear the voice of God in his life. He said this purification process was painful at first. He wept in sorrow over the sinful life he'd led, the women he'd hurt, the lies he'd told, and the time he'd wasted pursuing his own glory instead of glorifying God.

Eduardo worked on putting his faith back at the center of his life. He read the Bible and spiritual books for inspiration and to educate himself on his faith. "I had no money to pay rent. I had nothing, but I had everything," he said.

Eduardo considered joining a church mission to serve the poor in the Amazon rainforest for two years as a way to cleanse his soul of past sins, but his priest told him, "Hollywood will be your jungle. It belongs to God, not the studios, and we need to take it back. You need to be the light in the darkness, because Hollywood has such a large impact around the world, and our Lord touched your heart here for a reason."

His priest advised him to use his talent and connections to make films with a positive message. Mother Teresa once said that we are not called to be successful, but we are called to be faithful to God. If success comes with being faithful, then thanks be to God. With that in mind Eduardo created his own film company, Metanoia, which is Greek for "repentance." His goal is to make movies that are positive and inspirational and also serve God's purpose.

Metanoia Films's first major movie project was *Bella*. This powerful drama with a positive pro-life message was made for three million dollars and took in more than forty million dollars worldwide. The best results of the film were the e-mails, phone calls, and letters Eduardo received from women who reported that the movie changed their lives. In addition, more than five hundred women contacted his staff to say the movie convinced them to have their babies rather than have abortions.

The success of *Bella* allowed Eduardo to make even more positive and inspirational movies, including his latest, *Little Boy*. As his resources have grown, so has his passion for using his talents for the greater good. His most remarkable creation may well be his international aid organization *Manto de Guadalupe* (Mantle of Faith) that promotes human dignity and relief for those suffering. His work there includes mission trips to places where there is great need, including the Sudan (Darfur), Haiti, and Peru.

Another of his guiding passions is to steer young women away from abortions. He is so dedicated to this that he began spending his free time on watch outside abortion clinics in the poorest areas of Los Angeles. There, he would intercept and talk to pregnant girls and women, offering them solutions and helping them with medical care, food, and jobs. His efforts to put faith into action do not end there. Through his Mantle of Faith organization and tireless fund-raising, Eduardo built a medical center in Los Angeles that provides free high-quality care for pregnant women and their unborn babies. It is situated in a Latino barrio area that has ten abortion facilities within a one-mile radius.

"It drove me crazy and gave me headaches to see how many abortion places were in this Latino barrio, and after a year of being there on Saturdays to encourage women not to get abortions, I decided to provide them with an alternative that would help them deliver their babies and care for them," he said.

Eduardo overcame huge obstacles to make this vision for a medical center come true. I'm honored to have appeared at fund-raisers to support the Guadalupe clinic, which has state-of-the-art medical equipment and a wonderful, caring medical staff. Eduardo designed the facility to be like a spa, so when women entered, they would immediately feel comforted and cared for. Already, they have saved many lives.

Eduardo and I consider ourselves brothers now, but back when we were filming *The Butterfly Circus,* he had to yell at me to get me to spit on him for our big scene together. I kept begging the director just to do it with special effects. Eduardo, the professional actor, kept egging me on until I finally agreed to do it—of course, he wasn't so thrilled that an amateur actor had to do it seven or eight times before he got it right! They actually had to give me special tablets so I could work up a frothy spit.

I'm grateful that Eduardo did not hold it against me and that our friendship has grown over the years. He recently completed a movie titled *Cristiada* about a Catholic rebellion against persecution in Mexico in the 1920s, with big stars including Andy Garcia, Eva Longoria, and Peter O'Toole. (In 2012 the film was released in the United States with the title *For Greater Glory*). Eduardo's career is once again on track, but now he is able to live in faith and in peace as he follows his passion for serving God's will by making positive, faith-filled movies.

When I first met Eduardo on the set of *The Butterfly Circus,* he stunned me by saying that he'd kept a poster of me on the wall of his apartment for inspiration during the most difficult period of his life. As he told me his story, I found that Eduardo inspired me instead.

My friend's return to grace is proof that it is never too late for any of us to discover our true passion and purpose, something that allows us to express all the blessings and love God put into creating us. No matter where you are in life, no matter how far you may have wandered from God's path, you can always return to grace. If you have yet to find your passion—or if, like Eduardo, you have lost your way—have faith, forgive yourself, and ask God to do the same. Then you'll be on your way to becoming unstoppable!

FIVE

Body Weak, Spirit Strong

RACHEL WILLISSON OF CRANBROOK, BRITISH COLUMBIA, LOST HER mother-in-law, her grandmother, her father, and her dog all in one year. The only positive development during that time was that she became pregnant with her second child, a blessing since she and her husband, Craig, conceived this second child easily after having struggled for years to get pregnant the first time.

Then, in November 2007, just two months after she'd lost her father, Rachel and her husband were told by a sonogram operator that something was not right with their twenty-one-week-old fetus. A radiologist was summoned, and after more testing, he told the couple that the baby appeared to have no arms and her legs were much shorter than they should have been at that stage.

"In an absolute weeping mess, I raced home and Googled 'babies with no arms and no legs,'" Rachel said. "On the screen popped up this incredibly cute blond baby boy with no arms and legs but with a soother in his mouth! I started to read about that child, now grown into a young man in his twenties, and I watched every one of his videos I could find. I couldn't tear myself away from the screen. I watched ten or fifteen of those videos, and as I watched one after another, calm came over me."

The fearful, negative thoughts that had bombarded her at first were gradually replaced by more hopeful and positive thoughts. *If this guy is okay without arms and legs, then my baby will be okay. He seems to really be doing well. He seems happy and upbeat. He travels the world. We can handle this; our child will be fine.*

"Everything he said in those videos calmed me and gave me peace. I realized God was settling my heart by telling me if Nick Vujicic could become a magnificent person, our baby could too!" she recalled. "God knew who to send me."

Yes, that "incredibly cute blond baby boy," was me, believe it or not. (Thank you, Rachel! That makes two of us who think I was awfully adorable.) After finding my childhood photograph, reading about me, and watching my videos, Rachel and Craig Willisson realized that their unborn baby could live a relatively normal life, even a ridiculously good life. So when their doctor suggested that termination was an option, their response was, "No, absolutely not!"

"I don't think I took a breath before I said no!" Rachel said. "We had tried getting pregnant for ten years before our first daughter, Georgia, was born, and I could not even fathom the thought of killing this baby, Brooke. Maybe in society's eyes she was not perfect, but in ours she was. We realized that this baby was here for a reason—*God's* reason, not mine. Who was I to say what is considered perfect? She was kicking, moving; her heart was beating in my body. My baby, in whatever form, was mine."

Rachel and Craig decided they would raise their "little masterpiece" of a daughter just like my parents had raised me—"to do God's work."

When Brooke was born, her family was not only prepared, they were excited and feeling blessed. "We had a celebration," Rachel said. "They had to shut down the maternity ward because we had thirty-five visitors in our room with flowers and food and presents."

I met Brooke and her parents and sister two years after her birth. When Rachel told me her story of being at first overwhelmed by the radiologist's report and then calmed and reassured by my videos, I was so touched and thankful I couldn't stop crying.

My own mum and dad had no one who had gone through a similar experience to give them comfort and reassurance after I was born. But ever since I met the Willisson family, my parents have been there for them, offering their guidance and sharing their experiences. What a gift to be able to serve this family and their precious daughter Brooke, who was four years old as of February 2012.

"She is like a female version of Nick," her mother says. "They share the same determination and love and warmth, as well as this cheeky attitude with an excitement and zest for life that takes your breath away sometimes. But the greatest thing is hugging them. When you hug Nick and Brooke, because they have no arms, you get that much closer to their hearts. It always makes me sigh."

FINDING COMFORT INSTEAD OF DESPAIR

Brooke's father, Craig, is an example of something I have seen many times with individuals and families who've dealt with disabilities or serious illness. Instead of being angry or bitter about their child's lack of limbs and other physical challenges that have stressed the family's finances, Craig Willisson has drawn closer to God than ever before.

"I wasn't much of a church person or much into faith, but we named our daughter Brooke Diana Grace Willisson after the grace of God. Her birth definitely has brought me closer to God and to a lot of new people—our church family," he said.

Brooke's birth was a difficult one. Her mother hemorrhaged after the delivery. "But I saw how God stepped in and made everything right," said Craig, who decided to be baptized once his wife and daughter were both home and doing well. "I think God saw that Rachel and I are the type of people who can handle Brookie's disabilities," he said. "She is definitely a prodigy of God. And ever since her birth, He has helped us with a lot of good things. We recently had two 'angels' in our community pop up and offer to build a huge addition onto our place for free. We feel that God is pulling people together."

I stay in touch with Brooke and her parents, and the thing that always strikes me about them is that they are such joyful people. I don't say that lightly. They have challenges, to be sure, but you only have to be around them for a bit to realize how they truly have joy in their lives. Brooke is like a bright light that draws people to her, and her parents seem to always be celebrating the lives of her and her sister, Georgia.

Rachel has made a T-shirt collection for Brooke and their family and friends with messages such as "Who Needs Limbs When You Have God?" "When God Made Me He Was Just Showing Off," and my personal favorite, "Arms Are for Wimps!"

The Willissons have put their faith in action in dealing with Brooke's physical disabilities. They have accepted that God has a plan for their daughter, even though they don't know what that plan may be. They say it has helped them to watch God's plan for me unfold. They know that His plan for Brooke may be entirely different, but they are taking each day as it comes with gratitude, grace, and—as the T-shirts indicate—healthy doses of humor.

Why is it that some people with disabilities like Brooke or others with serious illnesses or cruel diseases can find peace, enjoy other aspects of their lives, and even make positive contributions despite their own challenges? Could it be that they have not allowed their physical problems to cripple them emotionally? Could it be that they've chosen to focus on what is good in their lives instead of what is bad? Perhaps. Here is another possibility: maybe they've let go and let God. Maybe they've decided to let go of their pain, anger, and grief and let God handle it instead. Most people dealing with serious health problems or severe disabilities put faith into action every day in some way. Often it is faith in their doctors and nurses or in their pills, treatment, and medical equipment. Accepting professional medical care is consistent with having faith. God has given you the opportunity to be served by trained and talented people. If you are thirsty, you might like to have it quenched supernaturally, but you surely would accept a cup of water handed to you by a caring person, wouldn't you? It's the same with God's leading your decisions as you walk in faith.

You don't have to be a spiritual person to put faith into action, but as a Christian, I have to say that knowing God is strong when I am weak gives me great relief and tremendous peace and joy. I can only wish, however, that I had the levels of joy expressed by my friend Garry Phelps who was born with Down syndrome. He is now twenty-five years old and one of the most inspiring people I know.

One day Garry heard some family friends talking about a newborn child who'd just been diagnosed with Down syndrome too. One of them wasn't aware Garry was listening when it was said, "Oh, that's so sad."

Garry jumped up from his chair and said, "Well, I think it's great!"

"Why do you say that, Garry?" the friend asked. "What is Down syndrome to you?"

"All Down syndrome means is that you love everybody and you never, ever hurt anybody!" Garry replied.

My friend has found the sweet spot in his affliction and in his life. Those with Down syndrome are said to have impaired mental capacity, yet I have to say that Garry may be wiser than many of us. He chooses to focus on the blessings of his burden and to give the rest up to God.

Garry leads a full and active life, writing, singing, and recording songs and exercising each day. I've never seen him "down" in any way. He loves Jesus without any doubt and with all his heart, and that is easily apparent in his beautiful and sincere prayers.

WHY ME?

Like most people with disabilities or serious health problems, I went through a long period when I questioned why a loving God would place such a burden upon me. It's a natural question and an important one. If God loves each of us, why would He allow anyone to be stricken with painful, life-threatening, and even fatal illnesses and diseases? Why would He allow so many, especially children, to suffer? Taking it further: how could a God who loves all His creations allow tragedies like terrible automobile accidents, earthquakes, tsunamis, and wars that maim and kill people? What about bombings, shootings, stabbings, violent assaults, and other grievous events that are all too common?

I asked those questions as a boy trying to understand God's ways, and I've been asked it many times by others seeking guidance. My lack of limbs draws others with physical disabilities to me, and many of them inquire how I've resolved those questions. Often they have far greater challenges than mine, such as cystic fibrosis, cancer, paralysis, and blindness. Most are looking for my answer to the "Why me?" question, but in some cases, they offer their own answers. I received an e-mail from a young man I'll call Jason, who had barely survived a terrible car accident.

He was riding in a car driven by a family member who lost control and struck the center median, flipping the car over. Jason's seat belt had been broken already, so he was thrown from the car. His skull was cracked, and his brain was damaged in four areas. He had some good fortune in that there was an emergency vehicle nearby. The paramedics saw his accident and immediately came to help. Jason had to have surgery to remove a section of his skull because his brain was swelling. He was in a coma for two weeks. When he awoke, the right side of his body was paralyzed, and he had difficulty speaking and smelling. A month into his recovery, his doctors discovered that Jason had broken his nose and collarbone. He spent another month in the hospital. He recovered his ability to speak, but his right side remained paralyzed and he had other challenges.

"I was afraid at first that no one would ever treat me the same," he said. "But then I had this sense that God was with me and that I would be okay. Ever since then my opinion about my injury has changed one hundred percent. I used to ask, *Why me? Why me?* But now I say, 'Why not me?'"

People have asked Jason if he still believes in God after so many bad things happened to him. "My reply is that God kept me alive. How could I not believe in Him?"

I'm with Jason. I don't believe God causes us to be hurt, sick, or to suffer a loss. But I do believe that God finds ways for us to use bad things for a good purpose. In Jason's case God kept him alive and strengthened him spiritually. Jason now places more value on every day of his life.

The Bible says suffering comes from Adam and Eve. We all have sin because of them. When Adam and Eve fled the Garden of Eden, they had fallen into sin and were banished from the supernatural world to the natural world. Because of their sin, they and all their ancestors—including you and me—were separated from God's kingdom. So while we seek eternal life through God in heaven, we first have to go through a temporary life in the natural world to get there. Still, while we are in the natural world, we should live with purpose so that God can bring the good out of even bad situations.

This is a difficult concept to master with logical thinking. A positive attitude is helpful, but it takes more than that to deal with a major medical issue. You need the love of your family and friends. And Christians can draw upon the incredible power of the Holy Spirit that transforms us from the inside out. As bad as your injury, illness, or disability may be, you can allow God to make something beautiful out of it. Personally, I can't make beauty out of pain and suffering, but in His mercy and power and greatness, God can.

God loves us just as parents love their children. Sometimes a parent intercedes when a child is hurting. Sometimes, though, a parent might not step in because the child needs to learn a lesson, figure something out, or pay more attention to the parent. There are even other times when a parent might step in to end a child's *happiness* because of danger or long-term threat—such as when a child is happily playing with matches or when a teen is enthralled with a boyfriend or girlfriend who is a negative influence.

God loves us and is not a hands-off Father. Thanks to our original ancestors, Adam and Eve, and their disobedience in the Garden of Eden, God's law is God's law. The crime of sin was committed, and the punishment was eternal separation from God. But that is not why He created us.

In the Old Testament you see animal offerings given as atonement for sin. Then God sent down His only Son, Jesus Christ, to die for the sins of men and women on earth so that someday we can all return to God's side in heaven.

Our Creator always acts out of love and with the desire to bring us to Him for eternity. The Bible says the wages of sin are death, but the gift of God is eternal life.

Sometimes God gives us His blessings. At other times, if He feels we need it, He may allow a challenge or a setback or something even worse into our lives to remind us to stay close to Him or to remind others through our suffering.

Yet there are also many loyal and devout Christians who suffer on this earth. What's up with that? I wish I had all the answers, but I don't. Some say that God may bring challenges into our lives to teach us humility, as in the case of Paul, the former persecutor of Christians, who wrote that when he became popular as an evangelist, God put a thorn in his flesh "to buffet me, lest I should be exalted above measure." But Paul noted that God also gave him the grace to bear that burden—something we can all hope for.

"Suffering produces perseverance; perseverance character; and character, hope," he wrote.

ADVERSITY BUILDS STRENGTH

I've always believed that God will put us through challenges to strengthen us. In recent years researchers in health psychology have found support for this in studies of people who've experienced severe stress and trauma across a wide range, from life-threatening illnesses to catastrophic events to the loss of loved ones. While you often hear about posttraumatic stress, psychologists have also found that those who deal successfully with health challenges can experience posttraumatic or adversarial *growth*.

Researchers found that many who successfully deal with physical adversity actually grow in positive ways:

- They realize they are stronger than they thought, and they tend to recover more quickly from future challenges.
- They discover who truly cares about them, and those relationships grow stronger.
- They put greater value on each day and on the good things in their lives.
- They become stronger spiritually.

The Bible's poster child for adversarial growth is Job. Satan took everything Job had, not only his land and possessions, but also his children and his health. Even so, Job persevered. In fact, he remained faithful to God, and in return God eventually gave him double what he had lost.

I believe there is yet another benefit that can come of major disabilities and health challenges. I think God allows some of us to be afflicted so that we can comfort others just as God has comforted us. This explanation particularly makes sense to me because I have experienced the truth of it time after time after time.

I don't claim to always understand God's plan. I do know that heaven will not be like this temporary life we are living. But it can be difficult to have certainty when God does something that seems harsh or unfair. You have to take comfort and strength from Him. You can make the decision to give the situation to God by putting in a request for His help.

The Bible says, "Be anxious for nothing, but in everything by prayer and supplication, with thanksgiving, let your requests be made known to God." Now, it may be impossible not to be anxious when dealing with illness, disabilities, or other life-threatening challenges, but you can find peace by putting things in God's hands. He can give you strength one day at a time, whether you need it for your own challenges or because you are grieving for someone else.

Know that whatever happens, there is no sickness or disease or death in the next life, but there has to be an end to all of us on earth. God's plan is not to keep us here to suffer and die; He wants us to be with Him in heaven forever.

Still, while we are here in our temporary lives, we have a beautiful opportunity to know God and to share His love with others who don't yet know that Jesus Christ died for their sins. While eternal life in heaven will be great, having a relationship with God while we are on earth is a tremendous opportunity.

Whatever circumstances you face, God will use you for His purposes. It may be years before you understand what that purpose might be. In some cases you may never know the full extent of His plans or why He allows some things to happen to you. That's why it is necessary to put your faith in action by knowing God is with you. Even though bad things may happen, they do not change the fact that He loves you.

MIRACLES ARE POSSIBLE

I'm not advising anyone to give up, of course. Miracles can occur. I've seen many myself, and people often share their own with me. John sent this inspiring story of his miracle, which also offers testimony to his faith in action:

I was not a religious person until about ten years ago when I looked death in the face. When I was young, I lost my leg due to cancer, and the doctors told me I would not live past five years old, at the very most.

Well, I beat their expectations, and on May 6, I turn thirty-seven. But it has not always been easy. The cancer comes out of remission once every several years, and last year it came back harder than ever. My doctors told me that unless I started a rigorous regimen of chemotherapy, I would die within the year.

I immediately shut them down and said I wanted to die and that I was tired of fighting. This cancer has killed my mother, two sisters, and three brothers, so I know it is going to get me someday. I was ready to go!

I spoke with my pastor about my decision, and after a lot of prayer, I decided to begin the regimen. I was scheduled two times a week for twelve weeks. Going into my fifth treatment, they did blood work and sent the results to my doctor as scheduled. Later that week he called me and asked me to come into the office. When I got there, he immediately came into the room and was actually crying. He told me that the cancer *was gone*! There was no sign of it anywhere. It's like it never existed. He was so happy, but not as much as I was!

I continue to get checkups every three months, and so far everything is good. I know someday it could come back, and I could even get hit by a bus on the way home from work. The fact is, we *never* know when our time on this earth will come to an end.

All our names and numbers are in the Book of Life. We just don't know when God will decide to take us home to be with Him. Love one another as if it's your last day on this earth. Live life to the fullest and appreciate every day that you wake up and take a breath.

John's story and many others like it that I've heard are proof miracles can happen. That is why I still keep a pair of shoes in my closet—just in case a miracle comes my way. You put faith into action by putting it in God's hands and presenting your request and praying for miracles, but if a miracle doesn't come, you can still be a light shining on earth for others. You can also do everything you can to learn more about God and by surrendering to Him.

Can God heal you? Yes, and that may be His plan. Or maybe it isn't. It is impossible to know, so walk in faith every day, knowing that God knows best. I have not received the miracle of arms and legs that I've sought, but I've experienced the miraculous joy and peace and trust of faith. That is more of a miracle than an illness cured. After all, you can be healed of cancer and still be miserable, taking everything in life for granted. By faith today I honestly have the joy of seeing lives transformed. This is *huge*! You may rejoice that you have limbs, but each day I rejoice that I do not.

The greatest miracle is a transformation from the inside out. So believe that a miracle will come, but know that even if it doesn't, God has a plan for you. The greatest purpose is to know God as a friend and to have the blessing of going home to heaven where no pain, no sickness, no hardship will ever find you.

I feel badly for those who don't believe in heaven. The thought that we only get one brief shot at life is pretty depressing. I want to live billions of years and into eternity. While I'm in this life, I try to have an impact that will last just as long. It won't matter how much money I've made or how many nice cars I've owned. What will matter is that I've reached out to someone and served a purpose greater than my own.

ARE WE A LESSON FOR OTHERS?

I don't believe God uses sickness to punish us, but I do believe He uses it to send a message that we need to hear. When His friend Lazarus was sick and dying, Jesus said, "This sickness is not unto death, but for the glory of God, that the Son of God might be glorified thereby."

When Jesus allowed Lazarus to die and then raised him from the dead, many doubters finally accepted that Jesus was the Son of God.

Could it be possible that our sicknesses or disabilities somehow serve God's purpose? I certainly have seen this with my lack of limbs, which has allowed me to serve others through my evangelism and also simply through my example. I think about how much easier it would have been on my parents if they'd known someone else with no arms or legs that could guide them and give them hope when I was born. I've been blessed to serve in that role for many men, women, and children with disabilities similar to mine. My parents have done the same, advising families and assuring them that their children without limbs can cope and thrive. If we do nothing else in our lives, to give some peace of mind and encouragement to others is a wonderful gift.

Michelle, a California mother, sent me one of the many e-mails that both confirm my purpose and humble me because I am reminded of how many people have overcome far greater challenges than I have. Michelle has triplets. One of them, Grace, was born at twenty-eight weeks' gestation with mild cerebral palsy, which affects her ability to walk. She also is blind in her right eye. Even with her physical challenges, Grace is a good student in mainstream classes, and even better, she has a strong faith. While Grace never seems to engage in pity parties for herself, Michelle has been asked the "Why me?" question.

You can hardly blame Grace or anyone for asking that when faced with severe disabilities or health challenges. I've often spoken and written about how my own mum responded to that difficult question. Michelle had read my first book and watched my videos, so she used her own version of my mum's response to guide her when Grace asked the "Why me?" question like I had.

"I told her, 'Because God will use you somewhere, when the time is right, to inspire people to turn to Jesus Christ!'" Michelle wrote. "I actually told her it was a kind of gift—to know your purpose so early on. I know some adults who still fail miserably to find it!"

Michelle said Grace listens to my videos to confirm that message, and she takes my photograph to school to inspire other kids that "nothing is impossible with God at your side!" According to Michelle, Grace has a renewed faith and loves God very deeply, even with all her disabilities.

"I sometimes suspect I am entertaining an angel," Michelle wrote.

Miracles come in many forms. You'll have to excuse me for believing that God's use of me as a tool for helping people like Grace is a miracle of some kind. If this were the only time someone had contacted me with this sort of message, I would consider it the gift of a lifetime, but day after day the letters, e-mails, and messages come in. Many of the people send them to thank me, but really I have to thank them for inspiring me with their strength and the power of their unstoppable faith.

Some of their messages are just incredible for the way they demonstrate faith in action applied to illness and disabilities. Adrianna certainly blew me away. She is a twenty-five-year-old who, like me, was born without arms or legs, but she does have hands and feet.

"God has shown me how to thrive and to know that I'm an equal despite my severe limitations. Like Nick, I struggle every day with daily tasks, but with strength I look on the bright side of life.... Through Jesus, God gave millions of miracles and healings to the world. God is real, and as an example of *Him*, I'm one of *His* children."

Adrianna spent her first three years on life support because she had trouble breathing on her own as an infant. Like me, she has back problems, but she's had two spinal operations to insert steel rods on each side of her spine. Still, this amazing young woman focuses on her blessings rather than her burdens.

"I only have hands and feet, but I'm smart and have many great friends and family in my life. I also go to college so I can become a counselor. God does miraculous things in life, and I am one of the miracles. Life can be good if we choose it to be good," she wrote.

Adrianna has many challenges, but she has rejected bitterness and self-pity. She remains in faith, positive, and a force for goodness in this world. She inspires me, and I hope her words inspire you too.

God wants us to be happy and enjoy life, and whatever we go through daily, we will rejoice in Him greatly and for eternity. Everybody's different in his or her own way, but our Father sees us as equal and unique as separate individuals and beings, and that includes all His creations on earth.

Despite our differences and disabilities and so much more in life, including things we go through as a follower and believer in Him, we are His special children and creations made in His image.

As we follow Him, we are doing great deeds to serve Him and our community, and we are spreading the gospel and Word of our Lord God and His Son Jesus Christ.

So, is God real? Yes, He is real. He may not be seen in person, but He is seen in Spirit.

Afflictions as Lessons

In Psalm 119, King David offered lessons on putting faith in action when faced with afflictions and other adversities. David wrote that before he'd become ill, he'd gone astray and that it was good for him to be afflicted because it made him return to God's laws.

My parents taught me that I should love God, not so He will protect me or give me arms and legs, but because knowing Him will lead me to life in heaven and a full life no matter what. When you are stricken with illness, disability, or other challenges, pray to be closer to God so that He can do what is best for you. This approach acknowledges that you may not know what is best, but God does. It also acknowledges that you don't have it in your power to heal yourself, but God does. When you pray in that way, you are putting your faith into action by putting all your hope in God's promises, which include this one: " 'For I know the plans I have for you,' declares the LORD, 'plans to prosper you and not to harm you, plans to give you hope and a future.' "

It's always a good idea to pray and remind God of promises He's made to us. I recommend large doses of prayer each day. I think they are the most powerful medicine of all. And there are other things you can do while waiting for God to reveal His plans for you.

From my own experience I know that being disabled, very sick, or suffering from injuries can stir up fear. You may also feel isolated, lonely, and stressed out. My worst times were often those in which I chose to go off on my own rather than to be consoled and cared for by those who loved me.

Don't make that mistake. If there are people in your life willing to be there for you, accept their support graciously and with gratitude. Tell them that you hope one day you can be as good a friend to them as they've been to you, and then give them the opportunity to help you as much as they are willing to help.

If you aren't surrounded by family and friends who can comfort you, seek out professionals, a church, or other support groups. Your doctors and other health-care providers can help you find them. There are support groups for most major illnesses and medical problems, and there are also more general groups that can offer help in dealing with any serious illness.

One thing I would caution you about is that when you face an overwhelming medical problem, you may find yourself totally caught up in dealing with it, so being ill and getting healthy again are all you think about. Professional counselors say that it is important to accept and manage your illness, but it is equally important to remember that you are still *you*. Don't abandon the things you love to do or the people you love to be with because you want to focus exclusively on restoring your health. The health challenge has happened to you, but don't let it take over your life or damage your sense of yourself and the value you bring into the world. You are more than this challenge.

Some days will be worse than others. You may lose ground before you can move ahead. You may have to concede to the physical pain now and then, but don't give up emotionally or spiritually. Stay strong in your optimism and your faith. Keep your sense of humor and your mind sharp, and look for moments in each day when you can find peace and joy, whether it's just the quiet of early morning or the joy of having another day, perfect or imperfect, to share with the people you love.

When I write or speak and describe my life as "ridiculously good," I'm referring to the joy that I take in each and every day. Whether the weather is beautiful or nasty, whether things go smoothly or every bad thing imaginable hits, whether I'm home with loved ones or on the road among strangers, whether I'm feeling fit or sick as a dog, life is just *ridiculous*.

You can't expect every day to make sense. Sometimes your days are just comical. Other days are tragic. But for better or worse, in sickness and health, good or bad, it is just ridiculous that we are alive and breathing, isn't it? Life itself is a miracle. You and I only get one ride on what Shakespeare called "this mortal coil," so what will you do on yours? Will you allow poor health, a bad injury, or a disability to take even a drop of joy out of your one chance at life on earth? I suggest instead that you go for an upward spiral. If you are put flat on your back by health problems or slowed down by a disability, take the opportunity to make sure your priorities are in order, let those you care about know how much you love them, and strengthen your faith.

There is always the possibility that God has put this challenge in your life to make you stronger, more loving, more courageous, more determined, and more faith filled. So take that possibility and run with it. Your body may be down and out, but you can still let your imagination and spirit go wherever you want to go. Maybe you've been too busy to upgrade your account, bolster your character, and clear out the deadwood. Now is the time to read the Bible and other books that fulfill and sustain you between treatments or visits from the nurses and nurse's aides and doctors and technicians. Work on healing and strengthening those parts they can't reach. Decide that no matter what happens with your body, the rest of you—your mind, spirit, and soul—will come through this restored and improved. Ask God for that gift of faith.

No Recovery, No Problem

Of course, if you have a lethal illness or disability like mine, there is no recovery. There is just the rest of your life. You either bail out on the time you have remaining and succumb to self-pity, bitterness, and anger, or you accept the challenge and make the absolute most of this God-given opportunity to do your best while the clock ticks down.

I have received a fair amount of attention and appreciation for the way in which I've chosen to live and to serve others despite my lack of limbs, but there are so many more people out there quietly meeting the challenge of their own illnesses and disabilities with grace, courage, and inspiring faith.

Rebekah Tolbert was born with far more challenging health problems and disabilities than mine. She was born as a fragile premature baby, delivered under emergency conditions to a family haunted by domestic violence. She weighed less than three pounds at birth but clung ferociously to life. Yet each day she endured seemed to bring more challenges.

Eventually, Rebekah was diagnosed with spastic quadriplegic cerebral palsy. Her parents divorced, but her mother, Laurena, instilled Rebekah with the knowledge that her family and her God loved her.

Filled with faith, Rebekah grew up with an amazing spirit and a cheerful, positive demeanor. Rather than feeling like a victim, she became a conqueror of challenges and a healer for others. While still in grade school, Rebekah mounted her own campaign to raise funds for Afghan refugees. She collected pledges for donations based on each pedal rotation of her custom tricycle and then rode far enough to raise more than fifteen hundred dollars for her cause.

She adopted her grandmother's favorite Bible verse, Ephesians 3:20:

Photo courtesy of Glennis Siverson, www.glennisphotos.com

I'm shaking with cold but also with excitement on the Santa Monica pier in October 2010.
I was producing and singing the "Something More" music video.

Photo courtesy of Allen Mozo Photography

I loved surfing for the very first time and getting tips from Bethany Hamilton.

In Surat, India, in 2008, during a five-day period, 350,000 people came to hear me, and 80,000 made a decision to have an active personal walk with Jesus. This photo shows a crowd of 110,000—the largest I've ever spoken to.

In a heart-stopping moment in Colombia in 2008, the guy directly facing me explained that he was sentenced to prison for twenty-five years but that his AIDS would take his life sooner. With such joy on his face, he told me that he'd found Jesus and that I should go and tell the world that "this man is free and full of rejoicing."

On that same trip to India and in the same town, we visited a school. I loved playing a little soccer with the children, showing them how I write with my mouth, and then giving them a mini speech.

I always wanted to see the sphinx and the pyramids of Giza. The Egyptians gave me a president's access because they knew I wouldn't lay a hand on anything!

Here I am standing on the Great Wall of China. What a cool thing to cross off a bucket list!

I love the innocent and transparent interactions I have with kids around the world.

In China, I met victims of the Sichuan earthquake, and this young man challenged me to race with him up and down the stage. Speaking to the thousands who lost their world in the earthquake was such an honor. I came away humbled and inspired by their strength.

I had a great chat and hug with this gentleman in New York on the street that's been his home for many years.

There is *nothing* like hearing the depths of a soul crying with relief that there actually is hope for her situation…and that someone cares.

We all need hope and inspiration. I'm at a nursing home telling this woman that I'm jealous of her because she's closer to the finish line.

This was one of the most life-changing days I've ever experienced. I spent time with these women and heard their stories of being kidnapped and forced into sexual slavery. I also heard how the Lord Jesus changed everything for them and in them!

I can't sign with my mouth for too long as I feel my teeth move, but when I do, I know the recipients have a gift to help them never forget a day of inspiration.

My signature move! I love hearing the silence of the crowd just before I get up.

I love Daniel—what a champion he is! I visited his school and encouraged his educators to keep him on par academically with his peers. I learned that Daniel was even exceeding the level of his classmates in several areas.

What can I say? The most gorgeous girl in India!

On February 12, 2012, we said "I do," became Mr. and Mrs. Vujicic, and were united in indescribable love. Kanae is truly the greatest gift I have ever received, after my salvation and relationship with Jesus! Love you, baby.

"Now all glory to God, who is able, through his mighty power at work within us, to accomplish infinitely more than we might ask or think."

For a high school class project, Rebekah partnered with Wheels for the World and put together a community drive to collect used wheelchairs and other medical equipment for victims of the 2010 Haiti earthquake. Her positive attitude and enthusiasm for life won her many new friends in school. She reached out to people, and most of them responded to her out-going personality.

But then Rebekah experienced challenges similar to those that I had around the same age. High school is the time when you become aware of your differences, and then you spend the rest of your life realizing how much we are all the same. The teen years can be challenging for anyone, and they are especially challenging for those of us who have disabilities.

When your mind and your body are maturing and changing rapidly, there are chemical changes in the body that also contribute to heightened emotions. It's a volatile environment because your classmates and friends are going through the same changes. Everyone is trying to figure out how to fit in, where to fit in, and what the future holds.

At that age I came to the realization that there were just some things that my classmates could do that even with all my determination and faith, I could not accomplish. I also experienced bullying and cruelty from other students during my teen years. Even though it usually was just a thought-less comment or someone's lame attempt at humor, I struggled with hurt feelings and self-doubt.

Rebekah went through similar challenges. Entering high school brought with it new joys, new friends, and new challenges as well as the growing sense that she was different from the other kids. Most of her class-mates were drawn to her cheerful demeanor, but some were uncomfortable around her. A few made hurtful comments or rejected her attempts to be friends.

Those comments and rejections hurt. Rebekah tried to remain upbeat and cheerful, but she began to struggle with self-doubts and despair: *Why hasn't God healed me? Why does He allow people to hurt me? Why do I have to be stuck in this wheelchair and in this body?*

In her hurt and disappointment, she also questioned God's love for the first time in her life: *Are You sure You love* every *person, God? Are You sure it's not every person but me?*

There is nothing wrong with respectfully asking questions of God. As the Bible says, "Seek and you will find." It's only through inquiry that we find answers. The problem comes when we let curiosity and an honest search for answers fuel doubt and shake our faith. Just because the answers to our questions are not readily available does not mean they are not there. Faith requires that we sometimes have to wait for God to reveal His plan for us. Sometimes when we ask questions and seek answers, we realize that His vision for our lives is much greater than our own.

Unfortunately, it is also true that life sometimes unloads one disappointment and hurt upon another. As much as you and I might try our best to stand up to these challenges, we may fall under their weight.

Despite her determined efforts to do well in school and to be a leader in her class, Rebekah found herself caught up in a controversy when it came time for her senior class graduation. She had fully expected to be graduating, and she'd even planned on offering a prayer at the ceremony. But because of a technicality, the school board ruled that she was not yet eligible for graduation, and she was not allowed to sit with her classmates during the ceremony or to participate in it.

This was a cruel blow for Rebekah. She'd long dreamed of her graduation day and the role she would play in the event. She'd also dealt with a series of tragic losses beginning with the death of her beloved grandmother five years earlier, followed by the loss of nine friends to leukemia, Parkinson's disease, brain cancer, and suicide.

Rebekah felt overwhelmed by unrelenting grief. Depression darkened her spirit, clouded her thinking, and shut down her faith. The enemy of her soul gained a foothold. This normally dynamic young woman who'd spent so much of her time finding ways to help others suddenly lost all interest in living. Each day seemed darker than the one before. The negative voices haunted her thoughts: *You are such a burden. Nobody really cares about you. They all just pity the poor little crippled girl.*

Suicidal urges crept in. One day she found herself staring at the knife drawer in the kitchen and considering a plan to kill herself while her mother was out shopping.

Rebekah's loved ones tried to lift her out of this depression. Her mother insisted that she go to church one Sunday. Normally, Rebekah was the first out the door for services. Now she did not want to leave her bed. Her mother insisted. She was certain that God's hand was still on Rebekah. She needed to be in His house, among His people.

Laurena helped Rebekah out of bed, dressed her, and helped her into a wheelchair. They drove to church. Rebekah was silent, still locked into her dark mood. As they entered the sanctuary, her mother reached for a church bulletin. A page fell out of it, an insert announcing an event.

Rebekah's mother saw a familiar face on the page. It was someone whom her daughter had often looked to for inspiration before her depression. With tears welling up in her eyes, Laurena handed Rebekah the photograph of me and the announcement that I would be the featured speaker at the baccalaureate ceremony at her school prior to the graduation that she'd been blocked from participating in.

"Do you still think God has forgotten you?" Laurena asked her.

Rebekah had often watched my videos, and she'd even prayed that one day she could meet me, because she harbored a dream of inspiring others and sharing her faith too. I've often been told that just the sight of me has an impact on people. I wasn't always sure they meant that as a good thing! But in this case it was.

For the first time in months, Rebekah felt a light come on within her. A sense of peace fell over her, washing away the tormented thoughts and self-pity. She told her mother that she wanted to attend the baccalaureate ceremonies.

After I spoke that day, Rebekah and her mother came and talked with me. Laurena told me of her daughter's struggles, so I prayed with Rebekah, and we spent a few minutes talking in private. She shared with me what had been weighing on her heart. I understood. I told her I'd been there myself, and I reminded her of one of her own favorite Bible verses: "I can do all things through Christ who strengthens me."

"Let go of your worries about your disability, and put your faith and trust back in God's ability," I told her. "Put your focus back on Jesus. Let go and let God."

Why did God create me without arms and legs? Why did He put me in a position to speak hope into the heart of this remarkable but hurting young woman? I look forward to the day when I can ask Him those questions face to face. Or maybe by then His reasons won't matter, only the results will.

In 2 Corinthians 1:3–4, the apostle Paul said, "Praise be to the God and Father of our Lord Jesus Christ, the Father of compassion and the God of all comfort, who comforts us in all our troubles, so that we can comfort those in any trouble with the comfort we ourselves receive from God."

I am overjoyed to report to you that Rebekah graduated one year later, in the class of 2010. At the request of her classmates, she offered a prayer of dedication. You can be sure she touched many hearts that day and in the days that followed.

She now puts her faith into action through Formed for His Use, her nonprofit organization, and by helping others fulfill God's purpose in their own lives as well as her own. Rebekah, once comforted, is now a comforter. She offers guidance and inspiration to individuals and families dealing with their own disabilities. By following her heart she reaches out to those who are hurting, offering them the love of Jesus Christ and sharing the message of God's transforming power!

SIX

Winning the Battles Within

TERRI WAS TWENTY-ONE YEARS OLD WHEN SHE WROTE TO MY LIFE Without Limbs website about her "tortuous journey of self-harm." She'd become addicted to the high she felt when cutting herself. Her craving for that sensation was so strong that she slashed arteries and tendons, risking her life.

"It was who I was," she said of her addiction to injuring herself.

In my travels I hear many similar stories, and they are very concerning. Mental health experts say people who harm themselves by cutting or bruising themselves generally are not trying to kill themselves, but too often they endanger themselves. It is a coping strategy, but it's like putting a Band-Aid on a severed artery. Cutting doesn't cure or fix the real problem. Those who practice self-harm usually are seeking relief from intense emotional pain that, in their distress, they feel they can't escape any other way.

Terri and others say their urge to hurt themselves is an addiction be-cause most get an immediate sensation of numbing or calming that makes them keep doing it, even though they know it is harmful. Often they would rather hurt themselves than do more pleasurable things.

The practice of cutting has been described as screaming without words.

Terri wrote of the torment that drove her to seek pain as a relief from overwhelming feelings of worthlessness and self-loathing. Fortunately, this young woman accepted help from a professional counselor. She stopped before the self-destructive urges led to her death.

Thanks to counseling and her own determination, Terri had not cut herself for a year and a half, but then urges began to plague her once more, she wrote. Again, her counselor helped her manage those potentially lethal impulses.

As part of the renewed treatment, the counselor told Terri my story and suggested she watch my videos. In her e-mail Terri wrote that my own journey put hers in perspective.

"If I have learned anything from Nick's story, it is that no matter how hard life is, no matter how tempted I may be, I should be grateful. I should be grateful for the fact that I even have arms. I should be grateful that I have legs. I should be grateful for being able to type this with fingers. I should be grateful that I am able to feed, dress, and take care of myself with such ease," Terri wrote.

"Why would I destroy such a precious gift that God gave me with such a horrible act?" she added.

Terri's story was both scary and uplifting. It's scary because her history of self-destructive urges was all too familiar. It's uplifting because she wisely accepted professional counseling and followed expert advice that likely saved her life.

Still, I want to reach people like Terri before they do any harm to themselves or to those they love. I understand their mental anguish, but I know there are much better ways to deal with it than slashing their bodies to bring physical pain. When I contemplated and then attempted suicide as a boy, I was convinced that my feelings of despair were unique. I felt alone in my torment, but the frightening fact is that I was just one of countless hurting people around the world who consider, attempt, and succeed at harming themselves or ending their lives.

Because most cutting and other self-inflicted injuries are done in private, there are few in-depth statistical studies of self-harm, which can include scratching, biting, cutting, head banging, hair pulling, ingesting toxic materials, and burning oneself. One study of US college students found that 32 percent reported having engaged in these dangerous behaviors. Experts on self-harm estimate that 15 to 22 percent of all adolescents and young adults have intentionally injured themselves at least once.

The statistical records on attempted suicide and actual suicide are more readily available and even more alarming. Every year approximately one million people on this planet commit suicide. That amounts to one intentionally self-inflicted death every forty seconds. Suicide has become the third leading cause of death for fifteen- to twenty-four-year-olds, and the rate of suicides has increased 60 percent in the last forty-five years, according to the World Health Organization.

Just recently I spoke at a Washington, DC, high school where I asked students to close their eyes and then to raise their hands and close their fists if they had ever had suicidal thoughts. Nearly 75 percent of the eight hundred students indicated that they'd had such thoughts. I then asked them to leave their fists closed if they had actually attempted suicide. Nearly eighty students indicated that they had attempted to take their own lives. Isn't that scary?

Those who are overwhelmed by suicidal urges often feel they have no purpose in life or that their lives are barren of meaning. They feel the future is without hope because of their pain, whether it's due to a broken relationship, a medical issue, the loss of a loved one, or other challenges that seem insurmountable.

Each of us has unique burdens. I understand what it is like to lose hope. Even now, looking back on my own suicide attempt—as wrong as it was—I can understand the thinking of the despondent boy I was then. My lack of limbs wasn't the problem; my lack of faith and hope triggered my despair.

Since I'd been born without arms or legs, I never missed them. I found ways to do most tasks on my own. I had a happy childhood of skateboarding, fishing, and playing "room soccer" with my brother and sister and many cousins. Sure, every now and then there would be unpleasant poking and prodding by doctors and therapists. Most of the time, though, I didn't mind the favorable attention my unusual body brought. Sometimes even good things came of it. Australian newspapers and television stations did features on me, lauding my determined efforts to live without limits.

Bullying and hurtful remarks were rare until I reached an age when nearly all kids are subjected to similar torment on a playground, in a cafeteria, or on a bus. My self-destructive urges came when I lost faith and focused on what I could not do rather than what I could. I lost hope in the future because my vision was limited to what I could see instead of opening myself to what was possible—and even impossible.

No one should feel sorry for me. And no one should play down their own challenges by comparing them to mine. We all have problems and concerns. Comparing yours to mine may be helpful, but the real perspective you should adopt is that God is bigger than any problems any of us might have. I'm grateful that Terri and other people find a fresh and more positive perspective on their lives by looking at mine for inspiration, but that is not what I'm all about.

First, although I lack a few items on the standard limb package, I'm having a ridiculously good life. In fact, my youthful self-acceptance and self-confidence did not begin to crumble until I began relentlessly comparing myself to my peers. Then, instead of taking pride in what I could do, I dwelled on those things my mates could do that were beyond my abilities. Instead of seeing myself as enabled, I saw myself as disabled. Instead of taking pride in my uniqueness, I yearned to be what I was not. My focus shifted. I felt worthless. I saw myself as a burden upon my family. My future seemed without hope.

Negative thoughts and emotions can overwhelm you and rob you of perspective. If you don't shut them down, self-destruction can seem like the only escape because you can't see another way out.

If I feel dead, why not make death a reality?

I can only stop the pain inside by causing pain on the outside!

A great many people have fleeting thoughts of suicide or self-harm. What will save your life in these situations is to shift your perspective from yourself to those you love, from the pain of right now to the greater possibilities of the future.

When self-destructive and suicidal thoughts torment you, I recommend putting faith in action, whether it is a faith that you will have better days and a better life, or faith that those who love you, including your Creator, will help you through this storm. Jesus said the thief comes to steal, to kill, and to destroy, but He comes that we may have life—a *more abundant* life.

SHIFTING PERSPECTIVE

My attempted suicide around the age of ten ended when my perspective shifted from my own despair to the emotional pain taking my life would cause my family and other loved ones. That shift, from myself to those I cared most about, took me off the path of self-destruction and sent me on a walk of faith. Your actions impact others. Consider how your self-destructive actions might affect those who love you, those who look up to you, and those who rely on you.

Darren wrote to our website saying he'd lost his job and a relationship and he'd experienced a financial crisis in just one year. Thoughts of suicide battered him night and day. He'd fought the negative self-destructive thoughts by watching my videos and by thinking about his children.

"I could not bear the thought of my kids growing up without me," he wrote. He realized that every life is marked by struggles, "but all you have to do is pick yourself up, dust yourself off, and know that life is good and will go on."

Now, maybe you feel that no one cares about you. All I can say is that the One who created you cares so much that He has brought you this far. Don't you want to see where the rest of the path leads? You may not have a strong spiritual background. You may not consider yourself a Christian. But as long as you are living and breathing, there is a possibility of better days ahead. As long as that possibility exists, you can put your faith in it and go from there, one day at a time.

Do you fear I'm offering you false hope? Consider that I'm writing this, my second book, without benefit of arms or legs! And consider, too, that I'm writing this as someone who just eighteen years ago tried to take his own life. Yet, today, I am incredibly blessed as a twenty-nine-year-old man who travels the world to speak to millions of people, a man sur-rounded by love.

YOU ARE LOVED

God sees the beauty and value of all His children. His love is the reason we are here, and that is something you should never forget. You can escape the hurt, the loneliness, and the fear. You are loved. You were created for a purpose, and over time it will be revealed to you. Know that where you feel weak, God will give you strength. All you have to do is put faith into action by reaching out to those who love you, those who want to help you, and most of all to your Creator by asking Him to come into your life.

Reject self-destructive thoughts. Shut them off. Replace them with positive messages or prayer. Let go of the bitterness and anger and hurt, and let God's love into your heart. The spiritual realm is very real. The Bible says that, when we pray, angels come down from heaven and war for us against the principalities of darkness. This is Satan's army trying to deceive you and destroy you with lies and those little voices of negativity. No need to be afraid, for God hears your prayers, and no name is more powerful than that of Jesus.

Some people may let you down, and it may seem that some even want to cause you harm. God won't. He has a plan for you. It's called salvation, and take it from me, it's worth sticking around to see what He has in store for you both in this world and in heaven everlasting.

One problem I've seen with many people who are dealing with self-destructive thoughts is that they don't trust that our God is a loving God. Somewhere they've come up with a view of God as a vengeful enforcer poised to strike down anyone who doesn't follow His commandments. If they've made mistakes or not lived a perfect life—whatever that is—they feel they will never be worthy of God's love. That is not true! Our loving Father always stands ready to forgive you and to welcome you into His arms.

Jinny wrote to tell me she contemplated suicide because she did not feel God's favor. She is not alone, especially among other South Koreans. Despite a thriving economy, her country's suicide rate has doubled over the last decade, giving it the highest suicide rate among the industrialized countries.

Suicide is the leading cause of death among twenty- to forty-year-old South Koreans, and it is the fourth leading cause of death for all residents, behind cancer, stroke, and heart disease, according to news reports. Group suicides planned on the Internet are increasingly common. Recently it was reported that thirty-five South Koreans were taking their lives each day. Seventeen hundred committed suicide in one month (November 2008) as part of a wave of "sympathetic suicides" following that of a popular actress. That was followed by the highly publicized suicide of a former South Korean president who jumped off a cliff after leaving a note that he could not "fathom the countless agonies down the road."

The stress of school and work is often cited as a factor in private conversations with South Koreans, but there are social taboos about admitting anything publicly. Seeking psychiatric counseling is also seen as an embarrassing admission to a flawed character.

I often speak in South Korea, China, Japan, and India about my experiences with suicidal urges because of the high rate of suicides in those countries. When I speak in those nations, individuals often tell me they feel alone and hopeless. They don't seem to understand that God is forgiving and loving. Jinny wrote that she considered suicide many times "due to my severe life. I believe that God is faithful, good, and generous to others, but not to me." Jinny added she has "always failed [to kill herself] whatever I've tried. I thought God didn't care about me, and that He was strict, cold, and stern to me."

The Bible says over and over that we are to fear God, which doesn't mean that we should cower in terror or hide from His wrath. Instead, it is a call for us to show Him respect and obedience while acknowledging His greatness. The Bible also says "God is love." We should never forget that He loves us so much He sent His Son down from heaven to die on the cross. So while we should respect God, we should always remember that He loves us too.

He is waiting for you to let Him heal you. He does not have to heal you physically; He just has to heal your heart. He will give you peace, love, and joy. He hears your prayers, so keep praying. And remember that He may not answer your prayers the way you want, or at the time you want, but His grace is always sufficient.

When things in your life do not make sense, keep on praying. Ask God what He wants you to do, and let Him heal you on the inside. He understands that you and I are not perfect. We are works in progress, but we should let Him work within us.

Your peace will come with God's forgiveness and love. Has someone told you that you are unworthy of His love? My first suggestion is to get a second opinion! Ask your heavenly Father to reveal His kindness and love to you. Draw strength from my story if it helps, but know that if you are patient, you will emerge from your despair and find hope.

You may have difficulty understanding how He can love you. In the Bible, Job had the same problem amid all his trials and pain. He said, "If I go to the east, he is not there; if I go to the west, I do not find him. When he is at work in the north, I do not see him; when he turns to the south, I catch no glimpse of him."

But Job later realized God's love for us is always there. After admitting that he could not see Him, Job said, "But he knows the way that I take; when he has tested me, I will come forth as gold."

No matter what you've done in the past. No matter what hurts you have endured. God will heal you with His love if you accept Him. Jinny finally came to understand this when she stopped viewing God as a fearsome figure. She thanked me for helping her do this after reading my first book, *Life Without Limits*. I am grateful to have been part of her healing, but I was surprised when she said one of the keys I provided was my ability to laugh at my circumstances and myself.

She could feel God's humor in my stories. "I can come closer to God because He will make me laugh," she wrote. "I'm back to peace now. Peace is in my mind even though nothing has been changed."

Trust in God as Jinny did so that even if your hardships remain, your mind and heart will be at peace through that season. Again, take it one day at a time, and you will come through these challenges.

You Are Not Alone

When I was contemplating suicide as a boy, I made the mistake of keeping those dangerous thoughts to myself. I was in despair. I was angry with God. I felt that no one could possibly understand my pain. I kept my negative thoughts to myself because I was not thinking clearly, which is how tragedies like suicide occur.

Of course, I was not alone. I was surrounded by people who loved me, and when it came down to actually trying to take my own life, my love for them kept me from proceeding. The thought of hurting them and burdening them with guilt was too much for me to bear.

Once my parents learned of my self-destructive thoughts, they immediately stepped in, although they did not learn until five years ago that I had actually attempted to take my life. The night after I held my face underwater in the bathtub and then stopped, I told my brother, Aaron, that I would probably kill myself at the age of twenty-one because I didn't want to burden my parents any longer. He immediately told my father, who wisely did not overreact. Instead, he told me that I was loved and that my mother and he would never consider me a burden.

Over time the veil of despair lifted. I still had periods of gloom and occasional meltdowns, but suicide never again surfaced as an option. Now I have Kanae, and the thought of losing even a second with her is beyond imagining. But, as in so many things, I am blessed to have so much love in my life. Many of those who have thoughts of suicide or harming themselves don't have a support network of family and friends nearby or maybe at all.

If you are in that situation, please remember that you are not alone. None of us is. God, your Creator, is foremost among those who love you. I encourage you to pray to Him and to seek support. Talk to your spiritual guide, whether it's a pastor, minister, priest, rabbi, or any person dedicated to helping others in need spiritually and emotionally. You should not try to handle despair or dangerous thoughts on your own. If you don't have friends or family with whom you can share your burden, you can find help through your church, your doctor, a local hospital or school, or a mental health department.

There are also many resources for counseling and suicide prevention available online. Hal found me that way, and I'm very glad he did. Like me and many others in despair and contemplating suicide, Hal isolated himself. He later regretted that. "I didn't tell anyone, which I now see as my biggest mistake," he wrote in an e-mail. "Had I trusted someone else with the fact that I was suffering, I may have had the courage to seek help instead of slowly drifting closer and closer to a permanent solution to a temporary problem."

That's an important point. Your pain and despair will not last. You only have to look at my life to see that circumstances can change dramatically for the better. If you feel you have experienced the worst life has to offer, don't you want to stick around to enjoy the best? When I was a boy, I certainly never imagined the wonderful experiences and loving people awaiting me. God's best awaits you too.

Fortunately, Hal had the presence of mind to fight his suicidal thoughts. He turned to the Internet, which can be either a good place to go or a bad place to go, depending on where you look. In this case he came across an e-mail from his mother who had sensed that Hal needed encouragement. (Way to go, Hal's mum!) The e-mail he sent to me was simply titled "Wow!"

Hal wrote that when he watched my video that day, he broke down in tears. Then he asked himself a series of questions and came to a conclusion that may have saved his life and certainly changed it for the better.

"How could I have been so selfish? How could I have thought that committing suicide was the only answer? I have a loving family, clothes on my back, food and water in abundance; I'm enrolled at a university, getting an education some people only dream of. I have been in love, and I have seen amazing things…and I was about to let myself forget that. That's what Nick did for me. He reminded me that life is a gift, a privilege, not a right."

I love the last thing Hal said: "I have never been a very religious man, but I do believe in miracles. I am alive because of them."

I get choked up whenever I tell this story, even now as I write of it, because Hal's e-mail contained a link to one of my videos. Think about this: I was once in the same position as Hal. If I had gone through with my suicide attempt, I would never have made the video that helped deliver him from despair!

Now think of the good that Hal can do to help others in the same way. Just reading his story in this book will likely help many people. So his life now has more meaning than he had ever dreamed. The same is true of you! You can't imagine what God has in store for you. If you ever have urges to commit suicide or hurt yourself, do what Hal and I have done. Put your faith in action and give your life to Him instead. I often draw strength from Psalm 91: "If you make the Most High your dwelling—even the LORD, who is my refuge—then no harm will befall you."

A HELPING HAND

Hal reminded me once again that if you have not yet received the miracle you've been praying for, the best thing to do is become a miracle for someone else! If you have overcome your own self-destructive impulses, I encourage you to reach out to others who may be in need of someone to help them with their own similar challenges.

Maybe you have sensed that someone you know is in despair, perhaps a family member, friend, or coworker? One of the greatest things you could do is reach out so they know someone cares. The most common triggers for self-destructive thoughts are a broken relationship, financial problems, a serious illness, a personal failure such as the loss of a job or a flunked test, a traumatic experience like a debilitating accident or military combat, and the loss of a loved one or even a pet.

In the Bible, Paul said that he believes our sufferings are not comparable to the goodness or glory that will be revealed through them. My own trials with my disabilities are worth it just to hear another person say, "If Nick can do it, so can I." We can be gifts and even miracles for one another, living proof that there is always hope.

While you never know what is going on in another person's heart, there are warning signs to watch for if you sense someone could be on the verge of self-harm. If you notice the following behaviors, I urge you to be there whenever possible for your friend in need.

According to experts, the behaviors that can be indicators of deep despair or depression that might lead to self-harm or suicidal thoughts include
- unusual changes in eating and sleeping habits
- withdrawal from friends, family, and regular activities
- violent actions, rebellious behavior, or running away
- excessive drug and/or alcohol abuse
- unusual neglect of personal appearance
- marked personality change
- persistent boredom, difficulty concentrating, or a decline in school performance
- frequent complaints about physical symptoms, often related to emotions, such as stomachaches, headaches, and fatigue.
- loss of interest in favorite activities
- intolerance of praise or rewards
- giving or throwing away favorite possessions or belongings
- becoming suddenly cheerful after an episode of depression

There may be other indicators, and these are not absolute proof, but if someone you know has gone through a traumatic experience, be particularly alert if she or he repeatedly makes negative comments such as, "Life stinks," "The world hates me," "I'm a loser," or "I can't take this anymore."

True Friends

Often, individuals in distress don't want to talk about their issues. Don't push it, but keep the communication open without offering advice or judgment. Just being there for them, hanging out with them, and letting them know you care can make a difference. You don't have to solve their problems. In fact, you probably aren't qualified to solve their problems unless you are a mental health professional.

Kate sent an e-mail to thank me for reaching out to her best friend at a speaking engagement. But what impressed me was the way Kate stood by her friend, always being there for her even when it wasn't easy. She said her longtime friend "started to go off the tracks" when they entered their high school years. The friend was diagnosed with depression, and she was harming herself. She'd also lost her faith.

"The hardest part was that I didn't understand any of it," Kate wrote.

Often the friends and family of people in distress cannot understand why they are hurting so badly. The *why* may not be accessible because the individual who is self-harming may not consciously know why either. Or the trauma may simply be too great to share. I'm particularly impressed that although Kate didn't understand her friend's actions and emotions, she remained loyal to her even when her friend pushed her away.

"Through this whole time I was trying my hardest to try to help her through her depression. But since I'm a really happy person who lives life to the fullest, she didn't want to hang around me anymore, but I didn't stop trying," Kate wrote. "That year she tried to commit suicide twice, and it pained me so much that she thought that there was no reason for her to be on earth."

A month after the friend's second suicide attempt, I happened to speak at their school.

"I was sitting next to her, and she did not take her eyes off you the whole time. What you were saying must have clicked for her, because during your talk she smiled a real smile, the first one in so long," Kate reported in her e-mail. "After we finished, she insisted on seeing you and giving you a hug, which she did. After you left that night, she said that you had started to restore her faith in God."

Kate added that this marked the beginning of her friend's return from despair and self-harm. She wrote to thank me for "giving me back my best friend," but in truth, Kate's loyalty and devotion to her friend made the restoration of their friendship possible.

Sometimes it won't be easy to stand by a friend or loved one who is dealing with despair or depression. Your loyalty will be tested. You may feel hurt, slighted, or abandoned. I would never suggest that you allow someone to mistreat you. If that happens, maintain a safe distance, but do whatever you can to help. That may mean simply being there for those who are hurting, listening to them when they are willing to talk about their concerns, and assuring them that they are loved and valued by reminding them that other people care about them.

If you sense that someone is more troubled than you are equipped to handle, you should contact a guidance counselor, a trusted clergy member, or a medical or mental health professional and seek his or her advice on what to do.

Most communities have mental health and suicide hotlines you can call for advice, and there are many resources online, such as the National Suicide Prevention Lifeline (www.suicidepreventionlifeline.org), the Self-Injury Foundation (www.selfinjuryfoundation.org), and S.A.F.E. Alternatives (www.selfinjury.com). You can find them by searching online for mental health advice, suicide, self-harm, and psychiatric counseling services.

REACH OUT

I strongly advise you to consult professionals and experts in your efforts to help someone in danger of self-harm, but if the person wants to talk with you, please don't miss the opportunity to reach out. Not long ago, I spoke at a church and afterward I just wanted to go home. I was worn out and hungry, and it was freezing outside. We were heading to the car when I saw a young woman sitting outdoors in the cold. Her head was down and it appeared she'd been crying. I craved food, warmth, and rest, but God touched my heart and told me to go to her.

Natalie had been overwhelmed with thoughts of suicide. Only fourteen years old, she'd run away from home and traveled by hitchhiking. A stranger had dropped her off outside the church. Maybe it was a coincidence that I happened to be speaking there, or maybe once again God revealed His plan for not allowing me to end my life many years before.

Natalie poured out her heart to me. She felt her life had no meaning. She was so distraught she told me she intended to commit suicide that very night. I did not judge her or try to solve her problems. Instead, I shared my own story of feeling frustrations and pain as a boy. I told her that after I had turned my life over to Christ, He had revealed my path and purpose over time. I told her that I had once felt just as she did, but my life had completely turned around.

My words touched her. Natalie said she'd desperately needed to talk to someone who understood what she was going through without judging or condemning her. I told her there were ways to turn her sorrows into joy, just as I had done. I prayed with her. The pastor and the church staff counseled her and gave her the assistance she needed to return to her parents and a better life.

Today, Natalie is free of any urge to harm herself or to take her life. We tell her story in my video *Passing on the Torch* at the Life Without Limbs website. You can imagine how grateful I am that I did not simply get into our vehicle and go home that night. God led Natalie to me so that I could put my faith into action and encourage her to do the same. If you encounter someone who is in obvious distress, please find a way to help or guide him or her toward someone who can. You, too, can be a miracle for someone. What a blessing that is!

I am concerned that there are many others like Natalie who are not being helped. There is a lost generation out there in danger of harming themselves because they have no hope and no faith to put into action. Nearly three out of every five young Christians (59 percent) disconnect either permanently or for an extended period of time from church life after age fifteen, according to research by the Barna Group.

I want to help turn back that tide. The Lord has given me an even greater passion for reaching out to young people in need. I have a renewed commitment to challenge my generation to be on fire for the Lord Jesus Christ and to share my passion for Him. My goal is to share a hope that ignites at least one person each day, then that person can ignite another and another and another until the world is illuminated with His glorious light. I call this "passing the torch."

Jesus said, "You are the light of the world.... Let your light shine before men, that they may see your good deeds and praise your Father in heaven." I believe with all my heart that this is possible, and I hope you will never miss an opportunity to help a person in need.

Please understand, too, that sometimes the people who may appear to be hard cases—hostile to authority and difficult to reach—are those who most need your help. Jesus didn't minister to the rich and the righteous; He sought out the most wretched criminals and impoverished sinners and offered them salvation. When I speak in schools and even prisons, often those who respond to my message with the greatest emotion are those who at first look like they'd rather be anywhere but listening to this strange-looking guy who wants to talk about God.

Gina appeared to be a teen who didn't want help, even though she needed it desperately. Gina told me her story in a touching e-mail, describing a childhood of abuse and conflict. "My heart was cold, surrounded by a wall to keep everything out," she wrote. She began cutting and bruising herself at the age of twelve.

"Satan was whispering in my ear, telling me that pain was the only thing real. I really did believe it and tried to kill the pain inside with a pain I thought I could control," she wrote. "I tried to kill myself four times, but failed. I guess God wasn't ready to let me off the hook that easy."

Despite her tough attitude and emotional problems, Gina remained in her church youth group, which proved to be a great blessing, because that is how I reached her. I was invited to speak at her church.

"When you started to speak, I sort of listened but tried not to let myself get involved. It was impossible," she wrote. "Everything else faded away, and there you were, telling me that God loves me, telling me that I have a purpose, telling me that I can use my circumstances for Him, telling me that I'm beautiful."

My message that day, like most, was very simple and came straight from the Bible, but this fifteen-year-old took it to heart.

"When you said that being perfect on the outside doesn't mean anything if you're broken on the inside, I think my wall started crumbling," Gina wrote. "After that, everything you said knocked another brick off that wall, until I was sitting there, my defenses down, tears pouring down my face, and I was changed. When I prayed, my chains fell off and I felt free."

Gina said that my simple words gave her hope.

"Suddenly, I could do it; I could live; I had a reason to, because I'm special.... It might have just been another day in your life. But to me it was another day I didn't give up, and more important, the first day in a long time that I didn't want to," she wrote. "You reached out to me, not touching my hand with yours, but touching my heart with yours and with the love of my Daddy. My Daddy, the Daddy who will never hurt me or cause me pain. The Daddy who will love me for who I am, despite all my faults and flaws."

Gina is a realist who has been through some very difficult experiences, but I love that she is now putting her faith into action one day at a time with hope in her heart.

"I'm by no means done with the crap in my life, but it's a start in the right direction," she wrote. "With time I hope that I can learn to use my testimony like you do, to reach hurting people and let them know that they are not alone and that there is a purpose, that they are loved. You handed me one of the greatest things of all. HOPE."

If you are hurting like Gina was, please take her words into your heart and put your own faith in action. If you know someone in emotional pain who is dealing with self-destructive thoughts, reach out to them. Even a simple message like mine can give them hope for better days, and you may save the life of one of God's children.

Here are some resources that you might find helpful for yourself or someone else:

- *Kids Under Twenty One* (KUTO; www.kuto.org) is a resource for teens provided by teens. KUTO offers crisis prevention, suicide intervention, and support to the community through awareness education and outreach.

- *National Suicide Prevention Lifeline* (1-800-273-TALK [1-800-273-8255]; www.suicidepreventionlifeline.org) is a toll-free, twenty-four-hour suicide prevention service. Callers will be routed to a crisis center in their area. With more than 130 crisis centers across the country, the mission is to provide immediate assistance to anyone seeking mental health services. Call for yourself or for someone you care about. Calls are free and confidential.

- *Teen Line* (1-310-855-HOPE [1-310-855-4673] or 1-800-TLC-TEEN [1-800-852-8336]; text "TEEN" to 839863; www.teenlineonline.org) helps teens address their problems through a confidential peer hotline and community outreach program. Open from 6 p.m. to 10 p.m. (PST) every night.

- *ULifeline* (www.ulifeline.org) is an anonymous, confidential, online resource center for college students seeking information regarding mental health and suicide prevention.

- *CrisisLink* (1-703-527-4077; 1-800-237-TALK [1-800-237-8255], National Suicide Prevention Line; and 1-800-SUICIDE [1-800-784-2433]; www.crisislink.org) was created to save lives and prevent tragedies. It offers support to individuals facing life crises, trauma, and suicide and provides information, education, and links to community resources to empower people to help themselves.

SEVEN

Fighting Injustice

ONE OF THE GREAT JOYS OF MY LIFE IS VISITING WITH MY FRIEND DANIEL Martinez. I described in *Life Without Limits* how Chris and Patty Martinez of Long Beach brought their nineteen-month-old boy to a church where I was speaking in 2008. They were seated far back in the crowd, but Chris held little Daniel in the air so I could see that this precious child was born just as I was, with neither arms nor legs.

At that point Daniel was the first person I'd met who looked just like me. Talk about an emotional moment! I felt an immediate bond with the Martinez family. I couldn't wait to meet privately with them to give them encouragement and to share my experiences. My joy was compounded when my parents arrived from Australia a few days later, and they, too, quickly bonded with Daniel, Chris, and Patty.

Since then we have stayed in touch. Daniel has proven to be even more fearless and adventurous than I was as a child. God put me in his life to give him the role model that I never had, and I feel blessed whenever we get together. So you can imagine my concern when the Martinezes told me just a few months ago that Daniel, now a first-grader, was having trouble because of bullying from schoolmates.

This upsetting news hit hard and it hit home. No matter where I travel in the world—China, Chile, Australia, India, Brazil, Canada—young people tell me stories of being bullied, ridiculed, and harassed in school, on playgrounds or buses, and increasingly online. Nearly every day we hear a new report of a young person somewhere who has committed suicide or lashed out violently after being relentlessly bullied.

When I address school groups, I am often asked to speak out against bullying and to call for an end to it. Of course, this is a very personal issue for me. Bullies targeted me often in my early school days. By middle school I had many friends, but even that didn't stop the hurtful comments and meanspirited teasing.

There was one particular taunter, an older kid named Andrew, who really got to me when I was thirteen by yelling something crude at me every time he saw me. There is no delicate way to describe what he would say to me. Day after day, he'd walk by me and shout out, "Nick has no ——!"

It's typical of the crass comments some guys make to one another, and I might have been able to laugh it off if he'd only said it once. But this bloke was relentless. It was bad enough to be missing my arms and legs. Now I had this yammering dodo falsely demeaning my manhood at an age when young men are sensitive about such things. It didn't help that sometimes a few of his friends snickered too, making me feel even worse. Most of the other kids did nothing, which also bothered me. You'd think someone would have told this jerk to shut up, but no one did, and that hurt and angered me even more.

You should never allow a bully to make you feel badly about yourself. But I know that is easier said than done. Words can hurt even if you know they are untrue and just meant to get under your skin. This is especially true when you are confronted time after time in front of your classmates and friends—and they do nothing to stop it.

I always tell people that I'm armless but not harmless. There was a bully in grade school who pushed me too far, and I bloodied his nose by hammering him with my forehead. He was bigger than I, but my high school bully was much, much bigger than I. (By the way, Andrew is not his real name. So my Aussie friends needn't bother trying to track him down.)

Back then I was not aware of how widespread bullying was or how serious it could be. I just knew that hearing Andrew's taunts at least once a day was tying my stomach in knots and making me a wreck. After about two weeks of this verbal abuse, Andrew and his insults were the first things I thought of upon waking each morning. I dreaded school. I found myself avoiding him, which made me late for class. I couldn't think straight half the time. I was either worrying about running into Andrew or feeling angry and hurt about the latest taunt he had yelled out in the corridor.

Some of my older friends offered to beat him up, but I didn't want to hurt this yahoo; I just wanted to shut him up. Finally I decided to confront him. I took the energy from my anger and fear and used it to power my wheelchair right up to him one day in the hallway after he'd shouted out his usual insult and embarrassed me once again.

Andrew looked even bigger at close range. This was one of those times that I wished my wheelchair was equipped with a battering ram, or at least a power hose. Still, I could see that he was surprised at my gutsy move.

"Why do you do that?" I asked.

"Do what?" he replied.

"Why do you tease me and say that?" I asked.

"Does it offend you?"

"Yeah, it hurts me every time you say it."

"I didn't realize that, man. I was just kidding around. I'm sorry."

His apology seemed genuine, so I accepted and we shook hands.

Just kidding!

In truth, I did say, "I forgive you," and that seemed to surprise him.

He never bothered me again. I'm sure Andrew didn't think of himself as a bully. Often, bullies don't. They think they are just kidding or teasing or trying to be funny. Sometimes people don't realize their words are hurtful.

But when they are, they need to stop or be stopped.

Andrew may have been one of those people who finds it difficult relating to someone with a disability. Maybe he tried to bridge the perceived gap between normal (him) and different (me) by teasing me. Whatever his reason, Andrew was hurting me and ruining my school days with his thoughtless remarks.

Those old feelings came back and caused an ache like old wounds reopened when Daniel's parents told me that he was being bullied in grade school. He and I are so much alike, not just physically, but temperamentally too. Daniel is a gregarious, fun-loving lad, and I knew that being bullied would steal his joy and trigger insecurities just as it had done to me.

So I offered to come to his school and talk to the students about the dangers and cruelty of bullying. The school officials rallied around the idea. They had me speak to all the classes from kindergarten through the fifth grade, and I was pleased to hear that the school staffers were doing whatever they could to help. They had Daniel speak to all the students about what he can and cannot do, how he does certain tasks, and what his life is like without arms or legs.

Daniel Day was a slam dunk. I made it clear to everyone at his school that I was Daniel's good friend and biggest booster and that I would take it personally if anyone ever bullied him again. I told them to be cool, not cruel. Beyond that, I spoke about the dangers and cruelty of bullying from my perspective and from a global view. I also talked about the impact of bullying on the victims and ways to recognize when someone is being bullied, and I encouraged all the students to speak out and act out to stop bullying in their communities.

A GLOBAL PROBLEM

My personal experiences with bullying did not end in childhood. Just recently I was traveling with friends and enjoying a swim at our hotel when an obviously drunk guy made loud and crude comments to me. It's a common misconception that bullying is a kid's problem. Tell that to the female police officer teased, intimidated, and shunned by her male coworkers. Or the elderly gentleman who lives in fear of the teens terrorizing his apartment complex. Or the teenager whose Facebook page is bombarded with crude and hurtful comments.

Bullying comes in many forms, ranging from name calling, teasing, and hurtful rumors to physical attacks and cyberbullying, which involves using the Internet, social networks, texting, and cell phones to harass and intimidate others. Most studies report between 25 and 40 percent of young people experience bullying in school. A National Education Association report in 2011 said that nearly all students have had some exposure to bullying by the time they graduate high school. That report added that bullying can result in academic, social, emotional, physical, and mental health problems.

Kerry Kennedy, president of the Robert F. Kennedy Center for Justice and Human Rights, has characterized bullying as a form of human rights abuse, and in 2010 the US Department of Education held the first federally sponsored summit to address bullying in schools.

Bullying isn't kid's stuff anymore. We all experience minor forms of harassment and intimidation as children. Playground teasing, however, has escalated in recent decades into more serious mental, physical, and emotional abuse that is conducted face to face and on the Internet and via cell phones. The World Health Organization has called bullying "a major public health problem" in schools, on the job, and in general society, where minorities and gays and lesbians frequently experience it.

Workplace bullying is every bit as prevalent and harmful as that encountered in the schools. This can include everything from verbal and physical intimidation to the spreading of rumors, shunning, stealing credit for work, backstabbing, and a boss who uses power to demand things beyond your job description. One study done by the Workplace Bullying Institute found that 37 percent of Americans have been bullied in the workplace and 40 percent never reported the bullying to their employers. Of those who have been bullied, nearly half had stress-related health problems, including anxiety attacks and clinical depression.

According to many studies, people who have been bullied or who have witnessed bullying are at significant risk of isolating themselves, abusing alcohol and drugs, suffering from health problems and depression, and injuring themselves. There also have been increasing reports of victims of bullies striking back with violence in which innocent people are injured or killed.

The normally peaceful nation of Finland was shocked in 2007 when an eighteen-year-old student massacred eight people at his school, including the head teacher, school nurse, and six other students. The killer, who shot some of his victims as many as twenty times, committed suicide after his rampage. He had taken five hundred rounds of ammunition to the school, and he had also tried to set fire to the building. A police investigation confirmed that he had often been bullied at the school. In a video posted prior to the shooting, he brandished a gun and wore a T-shirt that said, "Humanity is overrated."

Just a few years earlier, a California fifteen-year-old opened fire in a boys' restroom at Santana High School with an eight-shot revolver, and he then moved into the school's quad area. When his shooting spree was over, he had killed two and wounded thirteen. The shooter, Andy Williams, was small in stature and often bullied both at a previous school in another state and in his new school. The attacks weren't limited to his school, however. Someone had broken into his home, trashed his belongings, and stolen his Nintendo system. In his new hometown, his skateboard and shoes were stolen from a skate park, and just two weeks before the shooting, Williams was beaten up.

Bullying was cited in a 2002 US Secret Service report as a factor in 71 percent of thirty-seven school shootings studied by the agency. In several of those shootings, the attackers had experienced bullying and harassment that was "longstanding and severe." In some cases being bullied appeared to have been a factor in the student's decision to attack others.

This is a serious problem when you also consider that in 85 percent of these cases, there is no intervention by authority figures. Research also finds that a bully is six times more likely to be incarcerated by age twenty-four and five times more likely to have a serious criminal record as an adult. Experts say that today's school-yard bullies often become tomorrow's societal predators.

As a boy and as a man, my experiences with bullies have left me feeling intimidated, depressed, anxious, stressed, and sick to my stomach. The scary thing is that mine have been mild cases compared to most. The bullying reports that flow each day into my e-mail box and web pages are truly disturbing, as are many of the stories told directly to me by people who attend my speeches or talk to me in my travels.

I had just finished speaking to a large group of students at San Fernando Valley Academy in Northridge, California, about this very topic when a big guy with graying hair and a goatee approached me as I was walking out.

"Nick, do you mind if I talk to you a minute?" he said, introducing himself as Jeff Lasater.

He had such sadness in his eyes, I asked him to give me a hug.

Tears welled up in his eyes as he thanked me for encouraging kids to stop teasing and bullying. I thought that was all he wanted to say, but then he told me that his son Jeremiah took his own life in 2008 because of constant bullying at his school.

His tragic story shows just how dangerous bullying can be and just how stressful and harmful being bullied is for anyone, no matter what age or size you might be. Jeremiah did not look like an easy target for bullies. At fourteen years old he was more than six and a half feet tall, weighed around 275 pounds, and played offensive lineman on the junior varsity team as a freshman in a high school of six hundred students.

Still, the truth is that bullies prey on vulnerabilities, and we all have vulnerabilities. Bullies figure out how to get to you. Sometimes they attack physically, but they can also torment their victims mentally or emotionally.

My bullies usually picked on me because I was physically different from everyone else. They made fun of me for my lack of limbs or because I could not do all the things they could do. I was an easy target, but in some ways, Jeremiah's size and gentle ways made him an easier one.

Jeremiah had two vulnerabilities that his bullies picked on. He had difficulty fitting in because of a learning disability, which made school especially hard for him. He also was reluctant to use his size to scare off his tormentors, because he'd been suspended for fighting in grade school. Instead of standing up to the bullies or asking his teachers or supervisors for help, Jeremiah withdrew and kept his anger bottled up. His friends called him a gentle giant but said Jeremiah's reluctance to fight, despite his size, made him a big target for some who picked on him to prove they weren't afraid of such a big guy.

A friend remembered that Jeremiah was tormented so much in class one day that he finally stood up and said, "Just leave me alone!" Once the bullies realized Jeremiah would not fight back, they picked on him even more. Friends said he'd been bullied since grade school, and the problem only escalated once he entered high school.

On a November day in 2008, someone threw chili on Jeremiah in the lunch line. Another student tried to pull his pants down, according to Jeremiah's father. Distraught, the young man fled to the cafeteria rest room and locked himself inside a stall. Then he pulled a handgun out of his backpack and shot himself in the head.

No one knew Jeremiah's emotional pain. Like many others who've been in distress over bullying, including me, this young man hid his growing depression from his parents and friends.

"I was concerned a year ago that he was slipping into the place where kids go quiet," one of Jeremiah's teachers told a reporter after his death. "I would rather see kids act out."

School administrators said that Jeremiah had actually been doing better in his classes and that he'd also been feeling really good about having his best game on the football team the previous Friday. But here is the thing to remember if you have ever picked on someone, or if you are aware of someone being bullied: you never know what might push someone over the brink.

Jeremiah probably felt good about his better grades and his improved performance on the football field. We may never know why he decided to take his life, but maybe when the bullying continued, despite all the good things he was doing, he felt that the bullies were never going to leave him alone.

There have been similar tragedies, including the January 2012 death of fifteen-year-old Amanda Cummings of Staten Island, New York, who was killed after stepping in front of an oncoming city bus with a suicide note in her pocket. Police discovered that she had been bullied at school and on Facebook by her classmates. A survey of the school a year earlier found that 80 percent of the students there had been bullied or threatened.

One of Amanda's friends wrote on Facebook that she hoped her death haunted those who "made Amanda feel like the world turned its back on her," according to media reports.

The mother of another student who has been bullied at Jeremiah Lasater's high school attended a candlelight vigil after Jeremiah's suicide and told a reporter, "There will always be bullying as long as no one does anything."

Bullying is part of the dark side of human nature, and it surely has been with us as long as sin has existed in this world. Jesus Himself was a victim of constant bullying from His enemies. When He was taken into custody, Jesus was questioned by the high priest Annas about His disciples and teachings. Jesus told him that He'd always spoken publicly, so nothing was secret. He said Annas should question those who'd heard Him speak about His beliefs. Just then, another temple official slapped Jesus in the face and said, "Is this the way you answer the high priest?"

I like that Jesus did not back down from these bullying religious persecutors. Instead, He demanded to know why the official had lashed out.

"If I said something wrong, testify as to what is wrong. But if I spoke the truth, why did you strike me?" Jesus replied.

I believe the lesson Jesus was teaching in this instance was that no one should give in to being bullied or persecuted. Instead, we should put our faith into action, stand against those who would intimidate and persecute us and anyone else, and demand to be treated fairly.

Maybe a little teasing or a practical joke will be the last straw, the final blow to someone you know who has been quietly suffering as Amanda or Jeremiah did. Do you want to be the person who lets that happen, or do you want to be someone who helps prevent a needless tragedy? I suggest that you put faith into action and join those who are standing against bullying, hazing, and other forms of social injustice, like racial or sexual discrimination, religious persecution, and human slavery.

Jeff Lasater told me that he is determined to do whatever he can to take a stand against the sort of bullying that led to his son's death. Shortly after Jeremiah's death, his father founded Jeremiah Project 51 (www.jeremiah51. com), a nonprofit organization that has become a major force in the battle to eliminate bullying.

This father believes that bullying is like cancer, and the only way to stop it is to cut it out. Jeremiah Project 51 (Jeremiah's football jersey number was 51) is dedicated to wiping out bullying one school at a time. The organization provides a toll-free phone number (866-721-7385) for students or parents to call if a student they know is being bullied. The hotline number allows the problem to be reported anonymously. Project 51 staffers then make a call to the school and ask for an investigation within twenty-four hours, and then they follow-up.

Parents may also call that number for help if their efforts to alert a school to bullying are ignored. Again, Project 51 staffers make sure the school addresses the problem. The organization, based in Winnetka, California, insists that schools with bullying reports have an educational program that alerts staff, students, and parents to signs of bullying.

Jeremiah Project 51 also has a mentor program so that students who are being bullied have a senior class member at the school who supports them and advocates for them with backup from the organization. Project 51 pledges to help students and parents deal with bullying, even if it means presenting grievances to local school boards.

You are lucky if you've never been bullied. Very few people go through life without running into at least one *bounce* (which is what we Australians call a bully). But there is a big difference between a single encounter with a meanspirited jerk and enduring long-term, malicious verbal or physical attacks. Andrew's tormenting and ugly taunts against me lasted just two weeks; Jeremiah silently suffered for a long time. Despite his size and strength, this lad endured serious harassment and physical attacks for several years, according to his father. His reluctance to stand up to his antagonists and his lack of a supportive group of friends only made things worse.

BE A GOOD SAMARITAN

Those subjected to lengthy periods of severe bullying tend to be loners and introverts with low self-esteem who are more inclined to flee than fight. It's also true that minorities and people with physical and mental disabilities are often the victims of sustained bullying, shunning, and other abuse.

When I was a lad, bullying was not considered a serious problem. Many people thought of it as a part of life or something that everyone learns to deal with. But the level of bullying has escalated around the world. People are dying because of it, and lives are being permanently damaged.

If you know someone who may be targeted, whether a friend, family member, classmate, or coworker, I encourage you to be on the lookout and to be ready to reach out. Experts say the common signs that someone is the victim of bullying include:

- increasing reluctance to go to school or work or events that peers attend
- refusing to discuss the day's events upon coming home
- torn clothing, unexplained injuries, and stolen items
- asking for extra money to take to school
- carrying weapons to school
- reporting headaches, stomach problems, and nervousness before leaving and upon returning home
- reporting an inability to sleep or having bad dreams
- increased problems concentrating
- major changes in eating habits, either more or less
- little or no social interaction with peers
- self-harming through cutting, scratching, hair pulling, or other means
- appearing fearful of leaving the house
- running away from home
- sudden drop in school or work performance
- dramatic darkening of mood before leaving and upon returning home

- negative and self-critical expressions such as being "sick of life" or "I can't take it anymore" or "Everybody hates me"

I know from experience that the victims of bullies often hide their distress and depression from their families and friends, either out of embarrassment or from fear of making things worse. Most can't see a way to escape their tormentors, which can lead to tragic consequences. That appears to have happened with Jeremiah Lasater and Amanda Cummings.

I didn't tell my parents when I was picked on, because I didn't want to upset them or to be a burden to them. I figured I had to either let it go or handle it myself. Victims of bullying *do* need help. Even though they may not ask for assistance, they may welcome any quiet efforts to alleviate the situation. One of the factors that hurt most about my encounters with my nemesis Andrew was the lack of compassion from schoolmates who witnessed his verbal attacks but did nothing to help me. I'm glad that I eventually stood up to Andrew and even more grateful that he backed down. But I often wondered where the good Samaritans were in those days.

The Bible tells us that "an expert in the law" once tried to test Jesus by asking, "What must I do to inherit eternal life?"

Jesus asked the expert what was written in the law.

" 'Love the Lord your God with all your heart and with all your soul and with all your strength and with all your mind,' " the expert replied. "And 'Love your neighbor as yourself.' "

The law expert then asked Jesus, "And who is my neighbor?"

Jesus responded by offering the renowned story of the good Samaritan in which a traveler was robbed, beaten, and left for dead on the road from Jerusalem to Jericho. Two people passed by without offering any help, but a third man, who was from Samaria, went to his aid. The Samaritan treated and bound the victim's wounds, put him on his donkey, and took him to a hotel where he cared for him. Before leaving the recovering traveler, the Samaritan also gave him money and promised to return to check on him.

After telling this story, Jesus asked the law expert which of the three passersby was a true neighbor to the robbery victim and he replied, "The one who had mercy on him."

To that Jesus replied, "Go and do likewise."

I urge you to do likewise.

The Bible also instructs us, "Do to others as you would have them do to you." This is known as the Golden Rule, and it is one of the most basic principles of Christian living. It goes hand in hand with the commandment "Love your neighbor as yourself" and with the assurance that as we treat others, God will treat us likewise.

FAITH IN ACTION AGAINST BULLYING

God wants us to do the right thing, and that includes never letting another person suffer if you can help it. The traveler found by the good Samaritan had been bullied, beaten, and robbed. Jesus didn't waffle on what He expects us to do if we find someone in that situation. As God's children, we are expected to help one another. Standing by and watching someone be harassed, pushed around, ridiculed, and marginalized is not Christian behavior, neither is it humane. Most people would not let an animal be mistreated like that, much less a human being.

The good Samaritan didn't just offer a word of encouragement. He interrupted his own journey, treated the wounds of the beaten man, took him to a safe place, and made sure he was taken care of until he recovered. The Bible offers no description of the robbery victim, and I think that's because Jesus wants us to be good Samaritans to anyone in need, whether they are like us or not.

With that in mind I encourage you to reach out to anyone you think may be a target. You can help without putting yourself in harm's way. If you fear for your own safety, go to a trusted teacher, administrator, boss, security person, or law enforcement professional and give them the information, then ask them to intervene. Because bullying has resulted in so much violence in the schools and the workplace in recent years, your concerns will be taken seriously.

Every case is different, and every person who is bullied has unique abilities for dealing or not dealing with it. Most experts advise against physical confrontations if you can help it. Even if you win a fight with a bully, there is no guarantee that will be the end of your troubles.

These are the generally recommended steps:

- Document the bully's behavior by making sure there are witnesses, including authority figures, such as teachers, supervisors, security personnel, local law enforcement, or the human resources department for your employer.
- With friendly witnesses present, ask the bully to stop.
- Keep a record of the bullying episodes with dates, times, and places so that you can show a repeated pattern. Each time, write down how the bullying affected you physically, mentally, and emotionally. If the same person is bullying others, have them document it in the same way.

Cyberbullying and Texting Taunts

There is another form of bullying that has become prevalent with the increasing popularity of communication over the Internet and through texting on cell phones. This is generally known as cyberbullying, and even though the person doing the intimidating isn't present, this form of harassment is every bit as harmful as any other. Often, but not always, the bully involved may be harassing the same victim in person too. It's also not unusual for both parties to cyberbully each other with threats, rumors, and nasty comments.

Cyberbulling has been cited as a factor in a number of teen suicides in recent years. Ryan Halligan, a Vermont eighth-grader, took his own life in 2003 after rumors about him were spread on the Internet. His father described it as a "feeding frenzy" in which kids who normally didn't do such things were joining in the cruelty. In another high-profile case, Megan Meier of Missouri was allegedly driven to suicide in 2006 by online bullying from a classmate's mother.

Because of so many high-profile cases involving suicides and cyberbullying, many governments now have laws against using the Internet or cell phones to harass or intimidate others. If you feel someone is tormenting you with e-mails, social media posts, or text messages, there are many ways to respond. If you are living at home, you should alert your parents right away, so they can decide what to do.

If you are a victim of bullying, remember that the most important battle you must win is the one within. What someone else says or does to you should never define who you are. God created you for a purpose. You have value in His eyes. Put your faith in that, and then put that faith into action by rising above any criticism, gossip, or abuse that happened in the past. You were perfectly made by God. Don't let anyone tell you differently.

A bully wants you to believe that you are less than you are, because putting you down makes the bully feel superior. You don't have to play that game. Focus instead on building upon your gifts. God will take care of the rest. Joy and fulfillment will come as you walk the path created for you and only you.

ABUSE IN THE EXTREME

One way to move ahead in a positive direction if you have faced bullying or harassment is to focus on helping others and to make a positive difference in their lives, which I promise will make a wonderful difference in yours too. In my travels I've come across many dedicated and selfless people who've risen above their own challenges by reaching out to others. Some of them have been bullied and threatened for their efforts, yet they persevered.

As I noted earlier, there are many forms of bullying in this world. Anytime someone deprives another person of security, freedom, and peace of mind is essentially a human rights violation. Bullying is one form that is experienced by most people in some way. The most severe forms of human rights violations practiced around the world today include ethnic cleansing (also known as genocide), racism, persecution for religious beliefs or sexual orientation, sex slavery, human trafficking, and mutilation.

I've witnessed the horrors of human rights abuse in many forms across the globe. In *Life Without Limits,* I wrote of the "Street of Cages," the center of prostitution and sex slavery in the slums of Mumbai, India, where the Reverend K. K. Devaraj, founder of Bombay Teen Challenge (BTC), works tirelessly to alleviate the suffering of women and children from enslavement, physical abuse, poverty, sexually transmitted diseases, and drug addiction.

My ministry supported "Uncle Dev" in his extraordinary work in Mumbai, and I was delighted to learn of another Christian who put his faith in action at a high level to raise funds for Bombay Teen Challenge. In fact, this unusual fellow is both a Christian and a knuckleballer. In January 2011 major-league pitcher R. A. Dickey of the New York Mets raised funds and awareness for BTC during his climb to the nineteen-thousand-foot-high summit of Mount Kilimanjaro in Africa. Upon reaching the top after a forty-mile hike, he sent the message, "God is good." I appreciate what R. A. Dickey did in making Uncle Dev's great organization the beneficiary of his adventure, especially since the Mets told their star pitcher that if he was injured during his climb, it might void his $4.5 million contract.

There are many people around the world who put their faith in action to fight for human rights and against abuse of the weak and powerless. One of the most dedicated I know is an intelligent young woman who easily could focus solely on her career as a lawyer in California. I met Jacqueline Isaac, who is about my age, through her parents, Victor and Yvette. They are all dedicated and brave Christian evangelists doing God's work in the Arab world through their nonprofit organization Roads of Success. They produce an Arab-language Christian television show called *Maraa Fadela* (Virtuous Woman), which is hosted by Yvette and offers educational and inspirational material. Arabs around the world watch their shows by satellite.

Just a short time before I met Yvette, a disabled man in a wheelchair approached her outside her church in Egypt. He tugged on her sleeve and asked, "You are so focused on the needs of women and children. When are you going to start caring about *our* needs? We need help too."

Yvette felt badly but explained that she was not connected to any person or organization that ministered to people with disabilities.

The man in the wheelchair responded, "This is a message from God. He will bring you the person who will help you grow your disabled ministry. But don't be like the others. Do the work that is needed for us."

A week or so later a priest mentioned to Yvette that he'd seen a video of a young man who would make a great guest for her television program— me! She contacted Life Without Limbs and invited me to appear on her show. We became instant friends. I call Yvette my Egyptian mother. (No, not *mummy*!)

Although the Egyptian government at that time did not exactly welcome Christian evangelists into the country, Yvette is so respected that she was able to arrange a mission tour for me. My message about overcoming disabilities and other challenges was given wide coverage in the media and led to my meeting many government officials and leading personalities, including the mayor of Alexandria and the princess of Qatar, Sheika Hissa Khalifa bin Ahmed al-Thani, who works with the United Nations on issues affecting disabled people.

With the support of many influential leaders, Yvette helped me organize a 2008 event in which I hoped to speak (with her translating) to about two thousand people in Cairo. We were amazed when *twenty* thousand showed up, making it one of the largest gatherings of Christians in the nation's modern history. The success of that event opened the doors for me into many other Middle Eastern nations, including Kuwait and Qatar.

The Isaac family has embraced me and joined in my work on behalf of the disabled around the world. They do so many good things it is hard to keep up. They are also activists working to end traditions in that part of the world that suppress human rights, hinder education, endanger health, and oppress and harm women. In addition to their television and Internet ministry, they promote Christian concerts and evangelical events, sponsor mission trips, and conduct prayer initiatives.

Jacqueline Isaac, who is my unofficial second sister, is now a figure of international importance in her own right. She lived in California until the age of thirteen, when her life changed dramatically from a typical American teen's existence built around school, friends, church, and entertainment.

"When I was thirteen years old, I came home one night and found my grandmother dead on the floor. My grandmother was my entire life: she helped raise me, I fell asleep next to her every night, and she was always the person I went to with all my secrets. I was shocked! In fact, I was so scared, shocked, and angry that I started to blame her death on God," Jacqueline told me.

The teen was still reeling from her grandmother's death when her parents gave her even more shocking news. They had decided to move the family to Egypt, where they would continue their work as Christian evangelists.

"I had lost my grandmother, my life back home, and everything I was accustomed to," Jacqueline recalled. "It was then when I felt like giving up on life. I also remember giving up on God. I used to sit in my room by myself and shout out, 'God, if You're there, why would You take everything I know and love away from me?'"

Looking back, Jacqueline realizes now that she didn't understand that God had a much bigger plan for her life than she had ever envisioned. "In fact, one day I met with a pastor who was counseling me. This pastor looked at me and said, 'Don't you understand? God has stripped you away from everything that you know so that all you have left is to rely on Him.'" At that point Jacqueline understood God's calling for her life, and she knew she had to walk in faith, regardless of her circumstances.

"In essence, those difficult circumstances were exactly what I needed to shape and mold me for God's calling," she said. "I finally understood the principle of 'walking in faith.'"

Months after meeting with that pastor, another pastor was visiting

Egypt from Texas. She was leading a Christian conference. After the Texan's sermon, there was a segment of prayer time where she approached Jacqueline and said, "Young lady, God has called you for a high purpose. I see you moving around the globe. You will go back to the United States, but you will always come back to Egypt. I see you returning to Egypt many times and bringing the women and the people out of oppression. I see you speaking to people of very high authority and major leaders of the country. When you speak, they will listen, and God will give you anointing and favor. You will ask yourself, 'Who am I to have the honor to speak to these people?'"

Jacqueline was both shocked and humbled when she realized those words were a gift from God. "I had to hold on to His word and truly believe within that, even though I did not have the stature, education, or position at that point, God would do His work in me," she said.

At age fifteen Jacqueline was accepted by a US college, but she shifted from biology and plans to become a doctor after one of her mentors said she was destined to be an ambassador. "You are going to bridge the gap between two worlds, and when you speak, people will listen," he told her.

Jacqueline realized then that her destiny was linked to her parents' Egyptian homeland. "I knew God had a plan to send me back to Egypt. During my college years, I walked in faith and I allowed Him to do a wondrous work in me," she said. "Even when it sounded unbelievable, I realized when it seems impossible, hold on to the God who makes unrealistic dreams and wonders possible!"

Jacqueline has fulfilled that vision. She now works with religious and government leaders and social activists to bring change to Egypt. When she first moved there as a teen, Jackie was immediately struck by the oppression of women and shocked that even some of her female Egyptian relatives had been subjected to the horrific tradition of genital mutilation. When she questioned adults and even clergy about it, they denied that it was still practiced. Others said it was only done to "protect" young females from premarital sex. The United Nations Children's Fund (UNICEF) estimates that as many as 140 million women around the world have been subjected to this cruel cultural tradition, which remains widespread in Egypt, Ethiopia, and the Sudan, with some groups also practicing it in Kenya and Senegal. Many in those countries believe that this custom performed on infants to fifteen-year-olds is mandated by their religions, even though no major religion requires it. Others believe that this mutilation protects girls from sexual activity until they are ready for marriage.

"All I knew was that these girls had pieces of their bodies removed, and it was horrible," Jackie told me. "These things all shocked me. I could have been one of those girls if there had not been God's grace in my life. I was blessed enough to be an Egyptian American, and I felt an obligation to help the women of my country understand their rights and freedoms."

After Jackie returned to the United States to earn her law degree, she became an outspoken advocate of human rights in Egypt and across Asia, Africa, and the Middle East. She has made frequent trips to rural areas in Egypt and other countries in her campaign. Many times clergy and community leaders try to cover up or lie about these practices, even as young women are subjected to them in secret. When she learned that one clergyman was telling mothers in his congregation to have their daughters mutilated in this manner, Jackie confronted him. He told her, "It is better to cut your right arm off than have your whole body burn in hell," meaning that it is better for girls to have their bodies mutilated than to risk having sex outside marriage.

Since physicians and hospitals won't perform this illegal procedure, it is sometimes performed in barbershops or by midwives or clergy members. Infections, internal bleeding, and other long-term medical problems frequently result. My friend has put herself in harm's way by speaking out against this abusive practice and others, but she feels that it is necessary to put her faith into action on behalf of women and girls in nations where they remain oppressed and victimized.

"One time we were driving with a doctor and pastor to speak to three hundred village men, and my heart was beating a hundred miles per hour. He was petrified too. We knew there would be resistance, so I prayed to God, asking Him what I should say to these men. They had no idea what I was going to speak about. I was afraid they would kill me when I told them that genital mutilation was evil and dangerous."

Jackie believes that prayer is the tool to overcome all fear that may arise when you put your faith into action to stop oppression. She says prayer can bring victory beyond your circumstances.

"When I was about two minutes away from the church, I felt the Holy Spirit's peace coming all over me. This is when I knew that the words coming out of my mouth were not going to be mine, but it was going to be God speaking through me. It was God who would bring the victory. It was God who would bring favor over me, and it was God who would touch these men's hearts," she said.

When she stood to speak to the men, the mercy and grace of God fell over her. Instead of the feared outcome, a heavenly result took place, and God brought overwhelmingly positive responses from these men whom she had feared.

"They had their hands held up high. They were on their knees, begging God for forgiveness and repenting for their actions toward their daughters," she said. "All I could think was that if I had let fear control me, God wouldn't have used me in this unimaginable way."

Jackie explained to the men that many of their wives did not want to have sex because they'd been mutilated as girls and it was painful for them. Normally, it is considered offensive for an outside woman to even mention sex to men, but they responded by asking for forgiveness and vowing to never allow the mutilation again.

"I felt God was protecting me with His favor," Jackie told me. "It was very moving. We have seen so much repentance."

On another occasion, when she first began her efforts, Jackie went to a very poor and dangerous village to speak with women about their experiences with female genital mutilation, which was considered a taboo subject. Various people told her she should not go, "but I truly felt in my heart that God was leading me there. I felt Him say to me that it was important to tend to 'the least of these' in a village filled with thugs, trash, and poverty."

Jackie said she "followed the whisper in my heart" and went despite her fears. She was speaking with some women when two men walked into the apartment. One had a knife, and they started fighting with each other over whether Jackie should be allowed to stay. As they were fighting, the man with the knife fell down near Jackie's feet. "I began to pray and ask God to control the situation. I called in the name of Jesus, and all of a sudden, the man stood up, looked at me, and ran off," she said. Jackie called this "an incredible account of faith."

"I realized from this that when danger turns your way, it is because God is about to do something great that Satan wants to stop," she said. "The question is, how will you address the circumstance? By walking away or by facing Satan with the armor of Christ? I am so happy I stayed that day, because not only was I able to hear from these women, God used me to convince the father of the household to never circumcise any of his daughters again. In fact, this father began speaking to other men in his family and throughout the village as to how wrong the practice was."

In following the Bible's direction to "have nothing to do with the fruit-less deeds of darkness, but rather expose them," I have worked with Jackie and her parents to help in this cause with missions to Egypt and other countries, but this young woman's demonstration of faith in action under dangerous conditions is remarkable.

Since the Egyptian Spring revolution that overthrew the ruling party in Egypt in 2011, Jacqueline has become deeply involved with peacekeep-ing, consensus building, and human rights efforts there. She works with Christian and Muslim leaders as well as scholars, activists, and young revolutionaries to create a peace and human rights agreement, known as the Cannes Peace Accord and Plan of Action, for the nation. She has also formed a coalition movement called God Created All to unite Egyptians living around the world. In recognition of her work in Egypt, Jacqueline was asked by the world's highest sheik to be the US representative of the Family House, a committee organized by Egypt's religious leaders to en-courage cooperation between Christians and Muslims.

"The promise of God given to me as a young girl is coming to pass with every small detail today," Jacqueline told me. "Yes, it is dangerous sometimes, but it is like a fire in my heart. There is fear and concern about what I am doing, but I can't extinguish this passion, and after the revolu-tion in Egypt, there is a great window of opportunity to make a difference. So for now I walk step by step."

The Bible says, "He has shown you, O man, what is good; and what does the LORD require of you but to do justly, to love mercy, and to walk humbly with your God?" Injustices like bullying, hate crimes, religious persecution, and other human rights violations are responsible for much suffering in this world. I would never advise you to put yourself in harm's way, as Jackie has done, but if you are a victim, or if you know of someone who is being abused, please notify someone in a position to help. Put your faith in action against oppression and injustice in any way that you can. And most of all, pray for a world in which every individual is allowed to live unharmed and in peace while pursuing God's purpose.

Will you pray for yourself first? Pray that, if you are doing anything that can be seen as a seed of death through persecution or gossip or bullying, He would help you to change. Will you pray that God guards your heart when people put you down? Without prayer we are weak, but with it, we have His strength behind us.

Will you also pray with me that this generation will be the generation to stop being bystanders, that it will stand up to help instead? Pray for your school, pray for your bullies, pray for your heart that we may all remain alert for ways to make a difference in this world.

EIGHT

Letting Go
to Reach Higher

MY REMARKABLE FRIENDS GARY AND MARILYN SKINNER CAME UP WITH
a modest plan in 1983. They had already married and started a family in
Marilyn's native Canada. But Gary, who comes from a long line of missionaries and grew up in Zimbabwe, felt God's calling him to plant a small
church in war-torn Kampala, the capital of Uganda.

Their mission to plant a church may have been simple, but the decision
to leave the safety of Canada was not. Uganda was in the middle of a violent civil war in which hundreds of thousands were killed or displaced.
Guerrillas, thieves, murderers, drought, and sickness had transformed the
resource-rich country once known as "the Pearl of Africa" into one of the
poorest nations in the world. The chaos and strife of war was exacerbated

by a raging epidemic of HIV/AIDS, which had destroyed Uganda's social fabric as well.

Within just two years of opening their church, this dedicated Christian couple added another major task to their mission after finding scores of children wandering the countryside, abandoned in urban refuse piles and even bound and left to die. "We had the highest infection rate in the world at that time. I strongly felt God say, 'Look after My children,'" Gary told me when I visited with him and his wife and their three children a few years ago.

Marilyn said, "God wasn't impressed with how great our church was. He told us to look after the orphan children. The cries of children offend God greatly."

They began Watoto Child Care Ministries in a small rented house, but their ambitions were much bigger than any one house could contain: to provide needy children with homes, education, and medical care in a nation with an estimated two million orphans.

On a speaking tour in Africa, I visited one of the three incredible sanctuaries the Skinners have created for more than two thousand children. On their neat, beautiful grounds, groups of eight children live with a foster mother in more than two hundred homes. Each village offers schools and medical clinics with electricity, running water, and flushing toilets. These modern amenities, rare in most of Uganda, have been provided largely by volunteers from around the world who pitched in to help the Skinners' incredible example of faith in action.

Many of the children arrive at Watoto as newborns and remain through their teenage years, but the Skinners also provide financial support so that qualified young people can obtain secondary education degrees and establish productive lives. More than fifty Watoto children are pursuing advanced degrees now. Many more will follow. On average the village's baby-homes receive fifteen abandoned or orphaned infants a month. Many of those who come to Watoto are HIV positive, but treatment with anti-retrovirals and their mothers' antibodies usually clears the virus from their bodies, according to the Skinners.

The Skinners have had incredible success despite decades of continuous warfare, destruction, and atrocities around them. As recently as 2004, an estimated twenty thousand children were abducted by rebels who forced the boys to terrorize their own communities as guerrillas. Girls were raped and forced into sex slavery.

The motto for Watoto is Rescue, Raise, Rebuild. Their goal is to rescue the generation that has been lost to war, sickness, and poverty and to transform those who have survived into educated and productive Christian leaders equipped and willing to rebuild the nation. The Skinners also minister to the needs of the region's many impoverished and abused women through the Living Hope program, which teaches them life skills and offers vocational training and counseling to give them purpose, dignity, and a future.

Marilyn told me that they continued their work despite robberies, threats, and violence over the years. More than once they have courageously gone into the most dangerous regions to do God's work. A few years ago the Skinners undertook a mission into lawless northern Uganda to rescue some children enslaved by the rebel forces. Often the Skinners have not known how they would accomplish their enormous mission under such difficult conditions, but time after time they've put their faith into action and surrendered all to God.

"In the beginning we wanted just to plant our church and preach, but God said that He didn't send us to Uganda to do what we wanted. He sent us to do His work by serving the hurting people," Marilyn said. Even so, their church now serves more than twenty thousand members in eight locations. Their mission is still growing, because the need is enormous, Gary said. "But our God is great, and we believe that we can make a difference," he added.

Today, much of the world knows of the Skinners and their incredible ministry because of the performances of the renowned Watoto Children's Choir, which records music and travels the globe performing Concerts of Hope and raising funds so they can keep growing their mission to do not what they want but what God wants.

THE POWER OF SURRENDER

The concept of surrender can be difficult to grasp because most of us associate the term with failure, quitting, or giving up. When the Skinners surrendered their initial plans in Uganda to follow God's greater plan, they did not give up anything but the illusion that they were in control. They realized that God, in all His wisdom, had a larger vision for them, one that surpassed any plan they could have conceived in Canada.

Quitting would have meant leaving Africa and its millions of needy souls. Instead, they accepted that their heavenly Father knows best. They trusted God and said, "We don't know how we will possibly do what You want us to do, but we will trust in Your wisdom and rely on Your strength to fulfill the purpose You have designed for us."

You undoubtedly have to practice surrender in your own life—times when you have to give up trying to direct those things that are beyond your control and focus instead on doing your best, one step at a time, using all the gifts and talents and skills and brainpower at your disposal. You probably have done this without thinking about it. Maybe you've had to change careers because of the bad economy or a lost job. You didn't quit. Instead, you just accepted that circumstances beyond your control had changed the situation. You adjusted your plans based on the opportunities that remained, and then proceeded with confidence in your ability to survive and thrive.

What happens to you doesn't matter nearly as much as how you respond. As a Christian, my response is to let go and let God show me His plan. I can always tell when I'm out of sync with what He wants for me. In those times I feel frustrated, lost, and depressed—just like I felt as a boy approaching adolescence while trying to figure out how I could survive, let alone thrive, in a world designed for people with arms and legs. I was hung up on figuring out my entire life when God already had His plan in place.

Surrendering is about giving up the illusion that you are in the driver's seat. Yes, you do decide how you act, when you act, and the attitude you present to the world. Yes, you should dream and have goals for your life based on your passion. But it is an illusion to think you can determine what happens to you and around you. So all we really can do is prepare ourselves to manage the worst and do our best. That means developing our gifts to their full potential so that whatever happens, we have faith in our ability to persevere and plunge ahead.

The need to control everything around us can actually be a handicap. Here's an example that I can't do myself, but you probably can. Right now, clench your fist as tightly as you can. You have power over your hand this way, right? So if someone offered you the key to a brand-new BMW, would you pass up that opportunity just to remain in control, or would you relax your fist so you could receive the gift? It's the same with our lives. When we spend all our time trying to remain in control, we risk missing the blessings that may come by putting faith into action and letting go. If the Skinners had stuck with their humble dream to plant and minister a church in Uganda, they would have missed the far greater opportunity to have a positive influence on thousands of people and perhaps even the nation itself.

I would never advise you to give up on a dream, but I do encourage you to open up your life to the greatest possibilities and opportunities by surrendering absolute and continuous control. The whole thing about achieving victory through surrender is hard to grasp, unless you are married, of course. *I'm joking!* Well, maybe not entirely… I believe that when you commit to a loving relationship with someone, you surrender many things. You surrender selfishness and self-centered behavior. You surrender the need to always be right. And, of course, you surrender the television remote control!

On a deeper spiritual level, when you commit to a loving relationship with God, you surrender to His plan for your life, and suddenly the act of surrendering loses any and all negative connotations. Instead, it becomes a joyous and empowering experience. Many times I'm asked how I can claim a ridiculously good life when I have no arms and legs. My inquisitors assume I'm suffering from what I lack. They inspect my body and wonder how I could possibly give my life to a God who allowed me to be born without limbs. Others have attempted to soothe me by saying that God has all the answers and, that when I'm in heaven one day, I will find out His intentions. Instead, I chose to believe and live by what the Bible says, which is that God is the answer today, yesterday, and always.

When people read about my life or witness me living it, they are prone to congratulate me for being victorious over my disabilities. I tell them that my victory came in surrender. It comes every day when I acknowledge that I can't do this on my own. So I say to God, "I give it to You!" Once I yielded, the Lord took my pain and turned it into something good, which brought me real joy.

What was that something good? For me, it was purpose and significance. My life mattered. When I could not find meaning and purpose for my life, I surrendered the need to do that, and God stepped in. He gave my life meaning when no one and nothing else could provide it.

If you like word games, here's another way to understand what happens in my life each day. Put the word *Go* in front of the word *disabled*, and with a little creative visualization, you'll suddenly be looking at "God is abled." There you have it. I may be *disabled* but God is *abled*. He makes all things possible. Where I am weak, He is strong. Where I have limitations, He has none. So my life without limits is the result of my surrendering to Him all my plans, dreams, and desires. I don't quit, but I do surrender. I give up all my plans so that He can show me His path for me.

The Bible is filled with references to this, telling us, "I am the LORD your God who takes hold of your right hand and says to you, Do not fear; I will help you." Scripture also says, "I am the LORD, and I will bring you out from under [your] burdens" and "'I know the plans I have for you,' declares the LORD, 'plans to prosper you and not to harm you, plans to give you hope and a future.'"

In the Old Testament, God told Abraham to kill his son Isaac as a sacrifice to atone for sin. Abraham went along but did not tell Isaac. He just asked his son to accompany him to what Isaac thought would be a ceremony to sacrifice a lamb on the mountain. While they were walking up the slope, Isaac asked where the lamb was. Abraham said that God would provide it, but then, when they reached the mountaintop, the father told his son that *he* was to be the sacrifice.

Isaac did not fight back. He, too, surrendered to God's will, knowing that God's way is the ultimate way, no matter what we feel or desire. Fortunately for Isaac, this was a test of faith. As Abraham was about to stab Isaac, an angel intervened and stopped him.

There were two examples of surrender in this story because Abraham and Isaac both surrendered to God's will based on their faith. We must do the same in our lives, realizing that where we are weak, He is strong. In Scripture, God said, "My grace is sufficient for you, for my power is made perfect in weakness." So when God tells us to dream big, we can do so, knowing He can make it happen.

If you have surrendered in faith to God and life keeps throwing obstacles at you, tap into His grace and say, "If it is Your will to achieve this dream, help me." I believe God's path is the one that leads us to fulfilling our greatest potential. My advice is to know all you can and then surrender the outcome to His knowledge. Over time the puzzle will work itself out. As the Bible says, "His wisdom is profound, his power is vast."

You may be preparing to make a move, standing on the ledge but paralyzed by fear because you aren't sure *you* can do it. Try giving it to God instead. What will it take for you to trust this to Him? I encourage you to count the cost of what your life might be like without Him, without the Lord in all your decisions. Believe His promises for you today. Let Him be your joy and satisfaction. Ask God to be the One to define the purpose *of* your life *for* your life. Ask Him for the faith you'll need to do so.

When I released my bitterness over my lack of limbs, I didn't let it go for nothing. I had faith that God would step in. I believed His divine power would pull me through regardless of what I lacked. When I gave it to God, I felt a strength that was beyond me. The little faith I had was stretched beyond anything I thought possible. He has graciously let me be a part of changing people's lives. God changed me on the inside so I could be used as a chosen vessel unto Him to bear His name around the world. When I put my faith into action and surrendered my plans to Him, I began a new life of incredible joy and fulfillment beyond anything I could have imagined.

GIVING IT TO GOD

A few years ago a young woman told me her powerful story of surrender, one that surely will move and inspire you too. She began her e-mail in a very straightforward manner: "My name is Jessica. I am twenty-six years old now, and I was diagnosed with nasopharyngeal cancer when I was eighteen years old."

Jessica had graduated from high school in Pleasanton, California, and had just started her first year at California State University, Hayward, when she went to a doctor for a sinus infection that wouldn't go away. The doctor was surprised to find a large tumor in her sinus cavity. It was an advanced form of a malignant cancer that usually affects older Asian males. She was neither Asian nor male (obviously), but the diagnosis was correct. Her treatment was intense and painful.

This young woman was subjected to forty-five minutes of radiation a day, five days a week for several months in combination with about six months of chemotherapy. The radiation severely burned the inside of her throat, and the chemotherapy nauseated her continuously. She could not eat or keep food down, so her doctors had to feed her through a tube to keep her strong enough to withstand the treatments.

When Jessica was diagnosed with cancer, her dreams seemed to crash. She had to quit college in her freshman year and give up her part-time job because she was so sick she could barely get out of bed. The chemotherapy took her hair. The radiation burned her throat so she could not eat. Her pain was, in her words, "horrible, off the charts."

Despite her agony and suffering, Jessica chose that moment to put her faith into action through surrender. "It was during that time that my heart started focusing in the right direction," she said. "When you are that close to eternity, it makes you really examine your life to make sure you are right with your Savior. I wanted to make sure that my heart was truly committed. I did not want to just rest on some profession of faith; I wanted to make sure my life was backing it up."

I wrote earlier that God does not make us sick, but He does use illnesses and other major challenges to draw us closer to Him so that we put Him at the center of our lives. Sickness is part of the natural world; God's love is of the spiritual realm. You can see God at work in Jessica's life. Just as her serious health problems wracked her earthly body, He fortified her spiritual self.

"It seemed as if God were saying to me, 'Now that everything you relied on is taken away, are you still going to love Me? Do you love Me for what I give you or for who I am?'" she said. "At that time I made a decision to follow the Lord for who He was. I realized He wanted me to focus on what really counted in life, which was getting to know Him better, leading souls to Him and living for heaven."

The good news is that once she'd undergone her painful treatments, Jessica was cancer-free. Still, the cure took a toll that has hampered her speech and her ability to swallow food normally. Yet even with those lingering side effects, she surrendered all bitterness and self-pity and chose gratitude instead. "Glory be to God, I have my sight, most of my hearing, and—even though I have a harder time—I can still talk and sing," she wrote in her e-mail. "That is the physical aspect of what went on with me, but let me tell you the other side to my story, which is the message of hope I pray that I can pass on to other people who are in a similar situation as myself."

Because of her foundation of faith, the first thing Jessica did when her doctor found the tumor and sent her for an emergency CT scan was to surrender the outcome to God. She did not give up at all. Instead, Jessica gave her fight to God by tapping into the highest source of power available. She called the pastor of her church, and he organized an emergency prayer meeting that same evening.

In surrendering, "I had a peace that I cannot describe," she wrote. "Only God's children can understand the peace that I had. My whole world could have fallen apart at that very moment, but it didn't. The circumstances may have been out of my control, but Christ was still in control of my life. I knew He was going to be with me the whole way through. I knew that there was a chance that I could die. In fact, many times I went to sleep thinking it might be my last moment on this earth. I saw the reality of my circumstances, but I also knew the reality of my God. I knew that if I were to die, I would be entering heaven and I would be in the arms of the Savior who loved me."

THE PEACE OF SURRENDER

Take a deep breath. In... Out... Do you feel a sense of peace when you do that? We all long for that feeling of calm, don't we?

Our lives on this earth are not about what *we* want. You and I were created and placed in the natural world because of what God wants for us. He sent His Son to die for our sins, and Jesus made the ultimate surrender to follow His Father's plan to give us the gift of eternal life. As Jessica notes, there is an incredible peace in surrendering our lives to Him just as Jesus did. The Bible tells us, "Do not be anxious about anything, but in every situation, by prayer and petition, with thanksgiving, present your requests to God. And the peace of God, which transcends all understanding, will guard your hearts and your minds in Christ Jesus."

That peace can be yours only when you put your faith into action, surrendering your fears and any need to control your life, as well as any need to know the outcome of your actions. Instead, you put it all in God's hands, committing to follow His will. When you are searching for God's will in your life, whether it's trying to make decisions or looking for opportunities, you can't always expect a sign from God. Those are rare and wonderful occasions. What I've come to look for in trying to figure out what God wants is a *sense of peace.*

If serenity remains in my heart as I pray and move forward with a decision to act on an opportunity, I feel like I'm following His will. If I lose that sense of peace at any point, I stop, pray some more, and reconsider. I believe if I'm headed the wrong way, God will change my heart and guide me.

You may have many friends and advisors. Maybe you base your decisions on the alignment of the stars or a gut feeling. Everyone has a process. Mine is surrender. God understands us to the core because He created us. He feels what we feel, but His vision reaches those places we cannot see. There are many people I look to for advice and wisdom, but there is no one in God's league when it comes to guidance. I'm grateful to have opportunities, and often it seems like I'm walking down the corridor of a giant hotel with hundreds of doors waiting to be opened. It's difficult to know which doors are right for me, but through surrender, patience, and trust, God guides me.

Of course, God may say no to your plan one day, but the next day He may say yes to something even better. You don't know what God can do with your life until you give it to Him and feel the bliss in your relationship with Him. Whenever I become anxious about achieving *my* goals, I find peace knowing that I am here because God loves me and that He will be there when I let go.

Jessica has experienced similar results after putting her faith in action, which she says means "getting up and following Christ even when you do not see or understand His ultimate plan. It means finishing the race even when you feel like calling it quits. It means choosing to love even when it hurts. It means getting up and serving even at the times you feel the most weary." She adds, "Faith in action means looking outside of yourself to the souls around you who need to know that there is hope. It means trusting Christ to fulfill your needs and then getting up and helping fulfill the needs of others."

There is nothing quite as soothing as accepting that you don't have to work it all out, because God will. You can surrender yourself to Him and then wait patiently. Through Him, everything is possible. When Jessica was feeling her worst, she told God to do with her whatever He desired. Letting go gave her great relief, she said, because "I knew if my life was spared, then Christ had a purpose for it." There is tremendous peace, power, and freedom in that knowledge.

Jessica's cancer went into remission when she wrote to me six years after her original diagnosis. There was no sign of it in her body. She told me she was filled with gratitude even though her life had been forever changed and the aftereffects presented big challenges.

With her doctor's permission, Jessica returned to school and then to work. She became a medical assistant in a hospital's oncology and neurology departments, where she helped patients face the same challenges she had overcome. But after several years the work was too hard on her weakened body. She went on disability leave and now focuses on God's work.

"Going through the experience made me so grateful for what I have. It made me more patient and very determined. I am now on a mission, and I understand my purpose," she wrote. "My mission is to make sure people with serious health problems are able to experience the peace that I still have to this very day. This is the peace of knowing Jesus Christ as Savior. This is the peace that passes all understanding. The peace of knowing where you are going after you die. The peace of knowing that your life is in the hand of the Creator of the Universe. There is no safer place to be."

I heard from Jessica again just recently. It has now been more than eleven years since her tumor was found. She is still cancer-free, still grateful, and incredibly wise. Jessica has a much different perspective on her illness now. When she was first diagnosed, she thought God was punishing her for some reason. "I was looking at God only as a righteous judge, which He is, but I was forgetting that He is also a loving Father who only wanted the best for my life," she said. "I was only seeing His rod of discipline, and I was not looking at His hand of mercy and compassion. I saw it more as giving me what I justly deserved. The fact of the matter is that God was dealing with me with great loving kindness. He was taking the 'me' out of me and putting more of Himself in."

When you place your life in God's hands, you take the first step to becoming the person He intends you to be. There is great peace in that, and there is freedom and power too, because God works His miracles through those who give themselves up to His will. Jesus said, "If any man will come after me, let him deny himself, and take up his cross daily, and follow me."

Denying selfish interests—that is, shelving our own wants and desires and putting God first—is not an easy or natural thing for most people. Our earthbound bodies have powerful survival instincts that make self-preservation a priority. Even when we have a strong faith, the concept of surrendering all can be difficult to put into action and live every day.

Although she said the prayer of salvation with great sincerity at the age of fourteen, "I really did not know what it meant to live the life of faith," Jessica said. "I was still a very self-centered person. I thought the Lord was going to do things my way and fulfill all my dreams. At the time I had dreams of graduating college. I wanted to get married and have children— you know, the little 'white picket fence' life. I was very selfish, and I wanted everything that was going to make me happy."

Jessica believes that God used the illness of her body to strengthen her soul. She feels that being so sick forced her to focus on what being a Christian and giving her life to God really meant. Through her terrible pain and the loss of the life she'd known, Jessica found a path to wisdom and understanding beyond anything she'd ever experienced before. "God wanted me to realize that life was not given to me just for my own satisfaction," she said. "In fact, that is not the purpose at all. He wanted me to realize that life was given to me so that I could bring Him glory and be an encouragement for others. He wants the best for me, but He realizes the meaning of that more than I do."

THE MEANING OF SURRENDER

Jessica found that meaning through surrender. "The way I view it, to surrender means giving to the Lord the things that you hold most dear. It means not holding on tightly to your idea of what will bring you happiness but trusting that He knows even better than you know the desires of your heart—and that He will give you a fulfilled life even if it is not in the way that you envisioned," she said.

I don't know about you, but I am in awe of this young woman's wisdom as well as her faith. The Bible tells us, "Delight yourself also in the LORD, and He shall give you the desires of your heart." Note the psalm doesn't advise us to take delight in ourselves and give ourselves the desires of our hearts. Yet we often get caught up in trying to create our own happiness instead of giving our lives to God and delighting in His love and the life He created for us. Most of the time, when we try to make ourselves happy, we are just distracting ourselves for a while. You realize this is true when your happiness doesn't last or run very deep. A new car, a new dress, or a diamond ring doesn't bring you anything like the sort of joy that God can create if you delight in Him.

Jessica says she found the way to do this through "a life of daily surrender" even as she deals with the aftereffects of her battle with cancer. The intense pain of her cancer is gone. It is in remission, but now she has to live with the disabilities that have resulted from her disease and its treatment. Her speech is still distorted because her tongue and vocal cords are mostly paralyzed. She has difficulty eating and swallowing normally, and she is prone to pneumonia.

Her lingering physical problems could make for a difficult life—if Jessica chose to wallow in her misery. Instead, she chooses each day "to remember that Christ is in control." She told me, "I have to remind myself that the plans He has for me are plans to 'prosper me and not to harm me, to give me a future and a hope.' I have to surrender to the fact that even though I may not have the life I always dreamed of, I do have the life that Christ chose for me from before the world began. He has not made a mistake."

Like Jessica, I do not have the life I dreamed of as a child. I prayed for arms and legs because I thought they would make me happy. I thought that if I had arms and legs, I could take that deep breath and experience true peace. I believed that there could be no happiness for me without limbs. I didn't think I could ever create a happy life for myself, and I was right. My happiness came only when I put my faith into action and surrendered my life to God. He showed me that I am perfectly imperfect, just as He designed me. And He has provided me with more desires of my heart than I ever could have provided on my own.

Jessica is discovering the same in her own life. "The Lord has not brought me a husband yet, but He is daily showing me that He needs to be the love of my life," she said. "I do not have children of my own, but the Lord has allowed me to mentor several teenage girls, and I consider them my spiritual children. I hope that I can live my life as a testimony to them that God is alive and still works miracles."

As Jessica notes, you don't surrender your life to God and then expect each and every day to be all sunshine, flowers, and laughter. We live in the natural world, at least for now, and while sunshine, flowers, and laughter are part of that world, so too are blizzards, mosquito bites, and five-car pileups on the turnpike.

Surrender is a minute-to-minute, hour-to-hour, day-to-day process. You give it up to God every step of the way. In my younger years, I spent a great deal of time questioning God and His plan for me. Now, I am more patient, and instead of asking, I wait for Him to reveal His answers in His own time.

PATIENCE AND TRUST

Patience is part of the surrender process—and so is trust. You and I tend to want answers now, but we have to trust that God has His own timetable.

If we stay in faith and seek understanding, His plan will be revealed when we are ready for the answer. The purpose of a child born without arms or legs was a mystery revealed slowly as I grew in faith. As I've noted before, one of the keys for me was reading in John 9:3 about the man born blind. Jesus performs a miracle to heal him and explains that His purpose for this man was to use him to display God's glory. This scripture helped me realize that God might also have a purpose for me. Maybe, like the man born without sight, I'd been created without arms and legs so that God could deliver a message or somehow work through me.

As my understanding of God's ways and life's opportunities increased, He patiently put me on His path and opened my eyes to my purpose. Jessica said she has had a similar experience in dealing with her challenges from cancer and the treatments.

"I know for me there were times when I felt I could not go on," she said. "My voice is the one thing I have had a very hard time dealing with. I am hard to understand, and even though I may repeat myself several times, people may still not know what I am saying. It makes me feel very stupid and at times worthless.

"There have been days when I did not feel like opening my mouth, and I was angry that the Lord allowed my voice to be affected because it is something I have to use every day," she added. "The Lord showed me, however, that my voice is the very thing that gives me a platform to speak for Him. Because it is harder to understand me, people really have to take the time to listen. It also makes people realize that what I went through was real. It has given me several opportunities to witness and speak of what the Lord has done and is doing in my life."

I believe that when you surrender your life in full, with complete trust and patience, there is another great reward that comes your way: God's strength. Since the age of eighteen, I have traveled the world, often visiting twenty or more countries each year. I'm not flying in private jets. The places I travel to are often dangerous, difficult to reach, and unhealthy due to disease, impure water, and lack of modern medical care. Yet somehow God keeps me healthy and gives me the strength to carry His message to millions of people.

Jessica and I have both come to understand that surrender brings strength. "The times when I am the most weary are usually the times when Christ asks me to get up and serve the most. In helping others and seeing hopeless hearts find the peace of God, my own heart is then uplifted and I realize once again that the joy of the Lord is my strength," she said.

"So my suggestion to someone with tremendous challenges is to live life with a heart that is surrendered. Always remember that even though things may be hard here, Christ calls these our 'light and momentary troubles.' He says that they are bringing us an 'eternal weight of glory.' Look outside of yourself and reach out to souls that need the Lord and His love. In doing that, the Lord will fulfill your needs and make you see that He loves you beyond measure," Jessica said.

This young woman of God is incredible, isn't she? She told me that the Lord may come at any time, but she wants to be found faithful when He does. "I pray that I will be filled up knowing that my worth comes from Him," Jessica told me.

You and I may like to think that we are in command of our lives, our comings and our goings, but once we commit our lives to Him, God is in command every minute of every day. Our gracious heavenly Father often overrides my carefully made plans by revealing His own deep, unfathomable ways, and I am humbled every time. I marvel at the beauty and pure brilliance of God's divine plan each time. Sometimes I think back to what it must have been like to have been a disciple and an apostle and a witness to God at work through Jesus on earth, moving in indescribable ways. I can almost picture His followers returning to their own congregants scattered throughout the Roman Empire and reporting back to the believers saying, "You'll never believe what God did!"

The power of Jesus is here. When you put your faith in action by surrendering all to Him, you won't believe what God will do for you. I promise you will discover an exciting life when you put yourself in His hands. Look forward, then, to a life in faith, believing that Christ intends to use us as we intentionally surrender to His hope-filled, meaningful purposes for us. Allow His cleansing love to flow freely and at full force through your life. As the psalm tells us, "Taste and see that the LORD is good."

NINE

Sow Good Seeds

On my first visit to Liberia a few years ago, my goal was to inspire as many people as possible with a message of hope and faith. Given the country's reputation, I had no idea that this embattled African country and its long-suffering people would inspire me as well.

This small coastal nation founded by freed American slaves had long been known as one of the poorest, most violent, and most corrupt countries in the world. Although it was once among Africa's most educated and industrious nations and rich with natural resources, Liberia suffered greatly for more than thirty years due to political upheaval. Most damaging were two civil wars lasting until 2003. More than two hundred thousand Liberians were killed during that war. Millions more fled to other countries. Sex slavery and drug trafficking ran rampant.

The deep scars of violence and corruption were still very much in evidence when we arrived in 2008. Most of the roads were barely drivable. Electricity was rare outside urban areas, and even there it was sketchy. Only a quarter of Liberians have access to clean drinking water. Dead animal carcasses fouled the air and sickened our stomachs. Many people along our travel route appeared malnourished and destitute. Time after time, we saw men, women, and children rooting through trash bins and piles of garbage.

So you are probably wondering, where did I find inspiration in this bleak landscape?

Everywhere we went!

You see, the poverty and neglect we encountered are remnants of Liberia's haunted past—a dark period dominated by decadent dictators and bloodthirsty warlords. During our visit we also saw Liberia's future, which holds much hope.

For three decades few aid organizations, missionaries, or charitable groups dared to enter Liberia because of the hostile environment. But since 2005 that has changed dramatically. Billions of dollars are now pouring into Liberia, with the United States alone contributing more than $230 million a year to the rebuilding effort.

Our lodging host during my 2008 visit was one of the many charitable groups that have joined the international effort to help Liberia recover and rebuild. We stayed aboard the *Africa Mercy,* which is part of the Mercy Ships ministry. The ship itself is a former rail ferry that is now a love boat of another sort: a five-hundred-foot floating hospital operated by a Christian charity and staffed by a caring crew of more than four hundred volunteer surgeons, nurses, doctors, dentists, ophthalmologists, physical therapists, and other health-care professionals hailing from forty nations.

All those medical teams serving on the *Africa Mercy* donate their time and services, and most pay their own way to join its missions around the world. Liberia lost 95 percent of its medical centers during its civil war. While I was there, the state-of-the-art facilities onboard this amazing ship were some of the most modern in the world. On some days thousands lined up to come aboard and find help.

Africa Mercy is the largest hospital vessel in the fleet of this global charity. The Mercy Ships mission is to follow the two-thousand-year-old model of Jesus, bringing hope and healing to the world's forgotten poor by loving and serving others. In my talk to the four hundred volunteers aboard this incredible ship, I expressed my admiration for the great gift of their talents and skills to serve some of God's most needy people. The ship's volunteers give at least two weeks of their time, but some serve for many years. They actually pay for their room and board on the ship. That's amazing considering that these medical professionals are donating their only free time from their high-stress jobs back home.

I toured the ship and visited some of its six operating rooms, where patients were being treated for gangrene, cataracts, cleft lips, burns, tumors, broken limbs, childbirth trauma, and many other problems. Later, I learned that during the *Africa Mercy*'s stay in Liberia over the course of four years, the volunteer medical crew performed more than 71,800 specialized surgeries and 37,700 dental procedures.

The free medical care provided to the thousands of patients by the volunteers onboard the *Africa Mercy* is a wonderful example of sowing good seeds by putting faith into action in service to others. When I returned home, I raved about the volunteers so much to my sister, Michelle, who like our mum is a nurse, that she signed on for a tour with them!

Like me, my sister believes that we should all plant good seeds to grow strong trees that bear fruit for many years, creating more good seeds and more fruit-bearing trees in the process. Michelle and I may never see any of the fruit created by what we do during our time on this earth, but that's okay. Our job is to plant as many good seeds as we can, knowing that God will determine what grows and what doesn't grow. I encourage you to sow as many seeds of love, encouragement, inspiration, and kindness as you can.

The important thing with both love and faith is to act on them. Put them out there, where they can contribute to the greater good. It's a choice you can make every morning. Decide that you are going to use your God-given talents and abilities to serve a larger purpose. Each of us has talents of some sort, and we all have influence with friends and family and business networks that allow us to magnify our gifts by involving others so that they plant their seeds too.

We are here to follow the example of Jesus. The Son of God gave us His all, and we should give to God all that we have by serving His children with our love, just as we love Him. That's what Jesus did. He loved and served all of us even though He was the King, the Son of God. The great thing about planting good seeds is that God nurtures them as He sees fit, so sometimes the most humble seed can grow into something as large as a 16,572-ton floating hospital that has a positive impact on thousands and thousands of lives.

The Mercy Ships were envisioned and created by a Christian couple who acted upon their faith to sow good seeds and have served others in incredible ways. Living in Switzerland when they founded Mercy Ships, Don and Deyon Stephens have been recognized around the world for their humanitarian work, which provides the best in modern medical care to the poorest people of the developing world. Don holds a theology degree, and

Deyon is a registered nurse. They were inspired to refit their first mercy ship in 1978 after their son John Paul was born with severe learning disabilities. Later, Don was on a trip to India and met Mother Teresa, who encouraged the couple to join her in serving the world's neediest people. "John Paul will help you to become the eyes and ears and limbs for many others," she told them.

The Stephens were not wealthy, but they were so inspired by Mother Teresa's encouragement that they convinced a Swiss bank to loan them a million dollars to buy their first ship, a retired Italian cruise liner. Since then their charity has found support from donors around the world, including Starbucks, which put one of its shops aboard the ship to supply free coffee so the medical teams would have plenty of caffeine to keep their energy up. (Remember, what we can't do, God—and caffeine can!)

So there you have it, the first major source of inspiration I found in Liberia: a huge Danish ferry transformed into a ship of mercy by hundreds of wonderful volunteers, and a Christian couple who were inspired to serve others by the world's greatest example of servant leadership at that time, Mother Teresa. Through her selfless work among the poor in Calcutta and the missions she established in 123 countries, this humble woman inspired millions of people like the Stephens to sow their good seeds around the world.

You may ask, "What can I do?" or "What do I have to give?" The answer is, "Yourself." You and your God-given talents are the greatest gifts you can give. When you put faith into action to sow good seeds by serving others, you tap into a power beyond anything you can imagine. Just look at the lives saved and transformed by the Stephens and their mercy ships, or Mother Teresa and the more than six hundred missions she established around the world.

SERVING A NATION

The second major source of inspiration I found in Liberia was a woman like Mother Teresa, a servant leader and Christian of incredible influence. You may be surprised to learn that she was a politician in a country infamous for corrupt leaders. I was wary at first, but like other people around the world, I quickly discovered that Ellen Johnson Sirleaf was not at all like those tyrants and warlords who preceded her in Liberia.

In 2005 this Harvard-educated Christian known as "Ma Ellen" became this shattered nation's first woman president after having been imprisoned twice by a predecessor. At that time she was also the only woman serving as president on the African continent. Her election was hailed as a major move forward for a nation that had been plunging backward at a stunning rate. Former US first lady Laura Bush and secretary of state Condoleezza Rice attended her inauguration.

The new president had a tough job. She might have hoped to curb corruption and create jobs to put back to work the 85 percent of the population that was unemployed, but first she had to turn on the lights. After years of war, even the capital of Monrovia had no electricity, running water, or functional sewage system.

The daughter of the first native Liberian to be elected to the national legislature, President Sirleaf was well schooled in her country's cutthroat political system. She had accepted her scholarship to Harvard Kennedy School of Government in part to escape imprisonment for criticizing her country's corrupt leadership. When she returned home, she was imprisoned on two occasions for her continuing opposition. At other times she had to flee the country for as long as five years, working as an international banker during her exile.

The end of the bloody reign of Liberian dictator Charles Taylor began when thousands of Liberian women dressed in white, led by Sirleaf and the courageous activist Leymah Gbowee, gathered in a field in Monrovia and demanded peace. They stayed for months, through the torrid summer and rainy seasons, holding press conferences and bringing international attention to the human rights abuses of Taylor's regime. At one point the women protestors convened outside a hotel where Taylor's warlords were meeting and prevented them from leaving. Taylor finally fled the country. He was arrested and tried as a war criminal by the United Nations. In 2005 Sirleaf was elected to restore peace and sanity to her country.

When I met her three years later, Liberia was still struggling to recover from the decades of neglect and violence. For the first time in all those years, the Liberian people were no longer being victimized and persecuted by their government. The United Nations was helping to ensure the peace with a force of more than fifteen thousand troops.

During our twenty-five-minute talk in her office, I found President Sirleaf to be an impressive blend of strength and caring. There is a reason that she is also known both as "the Mother of Liberia" and "the Iron Lady." I was very nervous to meet her because I'd never before had a face-to-face meeting with the leader of a nation.

President Sirleaf welcomed me just days before her seventieth birthday, and her grandmotherly presence and the warmth in her kind eyes put me at ease right away. She also shared that she was among the 60 percent of Liberians who are Christians. She grew up a Methodist, and her early education was in Methodist schools. We spoke of faith, and I could see that much of her inner strength is rooted in her religious beliefs.

If I were ever to serve as any nation's president, I'd like to be like her. She is a woman of God who believes in a philosophy I'd characterize as

"Ask not what God can do for your country, but rather ask God what this nation can do for Him." What greater thing can a nation do than serve as an example of people trusting in God and handing Him their broken pieces to reassemble and repair. I believe this nation can serve as an example of the miracles God can do if its people abide in Him and His promises.

Since I was in President Sirleaf's country to speak to several groups, she asked that I encourage these Liberians to educate their children and also to return to growing their own food crops, especially rice, because the civil war had disrupted farming so much that the vast majority of rice consumed in the nation was imported. She impressed me with her powerful sense of mission to serve her 3.5 million people and to rebuild her ravaged country. Since she has taken office, Liberia has welcomed assistance from other countries and opened its doors to $16 billion in foreign business investments. On a personal level she seems very caring and attentive to others. In our case, before receiving us and welcoming us, she loaned us two SUVs so we could travel the rugged roads.

I don't have to make a case for President Sirleaf as an inspiring example of servant leadership at a high level. She's received one of the highest honors in the world for the seeds she's sown. Just a few years after we met, she and Leymah Gbowee were awarded the Nobel Peace Prize for their peace-building and human rights work. Four days after receiving that prestigious award, President Sirleaf won reelection for another six-year term so she can sow even more good seeds.

Sirleaf, who was also named the United Methodist of the Year in 2011, is recognized around the world as a benevolent, democratic leader—even as her predecessor, Charles Taylor, is being tried for horrible crimes against his people. Both of these people were in positions of leadership. Both were granted great authority because of those positions. Yet they wielded that power in vastly different ways.

One of the first Christian evangelists, the apostle Paul, discussed these two different types of leadership in the Bible, and the passage (Galatians 5:13–15) is particularly pertinent to a country created and run by former slaves and their descendants. He said, "For you, brethren, have been called to liberty; only do not use liberty as an opportunity for the flesh, but through love serve one another. For all the law is fulfilled in one word, even this: 'You shall love your neighbor as yourself.' But if you bite and devour one another, beware lest you be consumed by one another!" Paul was telling us that we should use our freedom and our power not to satisfy our own selfish needs and desires—or to fill our own pockets as Taylor did—but to love and serve one another as President Sirleaf is doing.

You don't have to be the president of a nation to serve others. You don't even need arms and legs. All you need is to put your faith, your talents, your education, your knowledge, and your skills out there to benefit others in ways big and small. Even the tiniest acts of kindness can have a ripple effect. Even people who think they have no power to impact the world around them can make a huge difference by joining forces and working together to become the change they desire.

Seeds Sown

President Sirleaf, Leymah Gbowee, and their army of women activists changed a nation by putting their faith into action to serve their people. They have helped to restore peace, and they are leading their country's difficult restoration after decades of strife. Just recently, Sirleaf put more than twenty-five thousand young people to work cleaning up their communities before the holidays and paid them so that they would have money for Christmas. Her administration has been busy building new health-care clinics and restoring water service to seven hundred thousand residents. Her major accomplishments so far also include the opening of more than two hundred twenty schools—a wonderful example of planting seeds that will grow and bear fruit for generations to come.

I was a witness to another sort of seed planted by the peaceful revolution led by Liberian Christians. This one is very close to my heart. My mission to Liberia included an evangelical revival meeting at a soccer stadium. We had expected maybe three hundred to four hundred people to attend, but to our joy an estimated *eight to ten thousand* came. People were literally sitting on rooftops and climbing trees to get a view into the packed stadium. Strangely enough, I had to give the same talk three times that day, because we only had one relatively small speaker box on the stage. So I had to aim it at one section of the stadium, giving abbreviated versions of my talk, and then redirect it at another section and give it again. I did that so everyone could hear my words of encouragement, hope, and faith!

That brings me to the third inspirational source I found in Liberia: the people themselves. Despite the death, destruction, cruelty, and incredible hardships they endured, millions of Christians in this nation have stayed in the faith. Even with many still suffering, I saw countless expressions of joy during our visit—from schoolchildren singing and playing, to stadiums filled with people praising God. Our friends in Liberia told us that Christians and Muslim leaders put aside their differences to help bring an end to the civil war through an interreligious council, and I am hopeful they can continue to work together for the greater good of their nation and its children.

I think I surprised my audience that day when I announced to them that I do not need arms or legs. After the murmurs over that remark quieted, I told them that what I really need is Jesus Christ. The point I wanted to make to these people who have endured so much oppression and cruelty is that, with God in our hearts, we are complete even when we would appear to lack many other things. I also assured them that while their lives on this earth have been extremely difficult, if they have faith and accept Jesus as their Lord and Savior, they will be guaranteed happiness in eternity. I also noted that even those who have everything on earth—including arms and legs—will take nothing to their graves but their souls.

I told them that they must have salvation in order to have hope. "Hope can only be found in God," I said. "I may not have arms and legs, but I fly on the wings of the Holy Spirit."

Then, I reminded my Liberian friends that God is still in control of their situations; therefore they must not give up but keep the hope alive. I told them that if God can use a man with no arms or legs to be His hands and feet, then He will also use war-torn Liberia for His purposes as well.

I reminded them that while we may not always receive the miracles we pray for, that does not stop us from serving as a miracle for someone else. Shortly after I said that, my words became a reality in front of thousands of people. As I neared the end of my speech, a Liberian woman came toward me with a fierce determination, working her way through the tightly packed crowd of people standing side by side.

Several times, security guards stopped her, but she quietly assured them that she intended no harm. As she drew nearer, I saw why they let her go. She was carrying an infant, just three weeks old. The child had no arms but did have tiny fingers emerging from her shoulders. I had the mother bring her child to me so I could kiss her on the forehead and pray for her.

My thoughts were only of showing love for this child, so I was startled when many people in the audience gasped and cried out when I kissed the baby. In the moment I thought it was simply because they were shocked to see a child with disabilities so similar to mine. Later, I was told that the Liberians were stunned to see a limbless child who'd been allowed to remain alive. In many villages children born with physical disabilities are killed. Some are even buried alive.

It was my turn to be horrified when my hosts informed me that children with disabilities in rural Africa were considered a curse. Normally, the child would be killed or abandoned to die, and the mother would be ostracized for fear that the curse on her would spread to her community. In the case of this child, the mother told us that she had fled with the child before anyone could take her away.

After I kissed the armless Liberian child, many in the audience realized that if God had a plan for a man with no arms and legs to be an evangelist, then this child and all others must also be children of God. One man in the audience told our security people that he was recording my speech in the Bassa language to share with a people who live in a remote, hard-to-reach area. He particularly wanted to tell them that I had said children with disabilities and deformities are also children of God, not a curse, "but an opportunity."

I can't absolutely confirm this, but I was told later that since my appearance and interaction with that child in Liberia, there have been no reports of disabled or disfigured children being killed or abandoned. I certainly hope that is true. I would feel blessed beyond belief if God used me to plant that seed, one that could save many, many lives and prevent great suffering.

VALUING ONE ANOTHER

Too much of our world is about seeking comfort instead of providing it. We can easily get so caught up in pursuing our own happiness that we miss out on one of God's primary teachings: true happiness comes in serving Him and His children. Jesus said, "For even the Son of Man did not come to be served, but to serve, and to give His life a ransom for many." Jesus was the ultimate servant leader and sower of good seeds, of course. God sent His Son to serve us with the ultimate sacrifice of dying for our sins. He presented Himself humbly, even washing the feet of His disciples to teach us that serving others is the best way to put faith into action. "For who is greater, he who sits at the table, or he who serves?" Jesus asks in the Bible. "Is it not he who sits at the table? Yet I am among you as the One who serves."

When we have God's love, joy, faith, and humility, we understand that no one human being is more valuable than another. I recently met someone who truly lives as a servant leader when I attended an unusual open-air church and ministry in downtown Dallas. Pastor Leon Birdd began his ministry with an incident that sounds like one of the parables told by Jesus. He was working as a carpenter and driving a truckload of furniture in a rural area outside Dallas in 1995 when he saw a middle-aged man walking along a service road.

At first Leon had no inclination to pick up the stranger, whom he thought might be drunk. But after he'd driven by him, he felt the Holy Spirit speak into his heart. He found himself turning his truck around and driving back to offer the man a ride. When this good Samaritan pulled alongside the man, Leon noted that he seemed to be having trouble walking.

"Are you okay?" he asked.

"I'm not drunk," the man insisted gruffly.

"Well, you're having a hard time. I'll give you a ride," Leon said.

As it turned out, the man, Robert Shumake, was telling the truth. He had difficulty walking because he had undergone several brain surgeries, which affected his mobility but not his determined efforts to help others in need.

For reasons that he never revealed to Leon, the gruff-talking Robert had been taking doughnuts and coffee to feed the homeless in downtown Dallas every Saturday morning for a couple of years.

"How do you do that when you can hardly walk?" Leon asked.

"People help me, and now you'll help me," he said.

"I don't think so. What time do you do this?" Leon asked.

"Five thirty in the morning."

"I am not going to drive you, especially at that hour," Leon said. "Even the Lord isn't up at five thirty in the morning."

Robert would not take no for an answer. He told Leon where to pick him up.

"You'll be there," he said.

"Don't count on it," Leon replied.

The next Saturday, Leon awakened at five o'clock in the morning, worried that Robert might be waiting for him on a street corner. He feared for Robert's safety since the location that he'd suggested for their meeting was a rough part of the city.

Once again, the Holy Spirit seemed to be working through him.

Before sunrise he found Robert standing on a street corner with a thermos filled with five gallons of hot coffee. Robert asked Leon to drive him to a doughnut shop, where they loaded up on pastries. They then proceeded to downtown Dallas. The streets were empty.

"Just wait," Robert told Leon.

With the big thermos of steaming coffee on the curb, they waited. As the sun rose, homeless people appeared one by one. Nearly fifty of them assembled for Robert's coffee and doughnuts. Although Robert had a rough way of talking to the people he served, they welcomed the warm coffee and doughnuts. Leon, who had given his life to Christ a couple of years earlier, saw that Robert was sowing good seeds and that he clearly needed help. So he began assisting him each Saturday morning after that. In the months that followed, Robert's health declined.

"Robert, what happens when you can't do this anymore?" Leon asked one day as they packed up.

"You'll do it," Robert said.

"No, you really need to get someone else," Leon insisted.

"You will do it," Robert said again.

Robert was right. Leon Birdd became Pastor Birdd, an ordained minister with an inner-city mission supported by nine local churches and other donors. Although Robert died in 2009, the seeds he planted have been nurtured and grown by Pastor Birdd and his wife, Jennifer. Today, those street-corner meetings for coffee and doughnuts are full-blown, open-air services with music and celebrations of faith. Now, every Sunday morning, more than fifty volunteers join Pastor Birdd in feeding the bodies and ministering to the souls of hundreds of homeless in a downtown Dallas parking lot.

When I was invited to speak at one of their services, I was inspired by the Birdds and all the caring and comfort they provide to those most needy people. The leaders and volunteers at Pastor Birdd's SOUL Church value every individual as a child of God. They understand that everyone needs love and encouragement, even if it is just a kind word or a smile to go with a doughnut and a cup of coffee.

Birdd considers himself the Lord's servant and says that many of those who serve at his open-air church have been either homeless or struggling in their lives. "Then they were touched with the grace and forgiveness that is found in Jesus. Therefore we love with no strings attached, as our Lord has loved us."

WORKING TOGETHER FOR THE GREATER GOOD

You can sow good seeds, no matter where you are in life, no matter what your circumstances might be. Whether you are the founder or a volunteer aboard a huge charitable operation like the *Africa Mercy* ship, a national leader like President Sirleaf, or the pastor of a ministry to the homeless, the godly work that you do is magnified many times over because of the countless lives you touch.

All the servant leaders I've met in my travels share certain characteristics and attitudes that all of us should adopt and emulate. First, they are incredibly humble and selfless. Many of them give their lives to the service of others, and they don't care if they receive any recognition. Instead of standing at the forefront, most would rather be at the back of the room, urging on their volunteers and encouraging those they serve. They would rather give credit than receive it.

Second, servant leaders are great listeners and empathizers. They listen to understand the needs of those they serve, and they observe and empathize to pick up on unexpressed needs. Usually people don't have to come to them and ask for help, because they've already detected what is needed. Servant leaders operate with these thoughts in mind: *If I were in this person's situation, what would comfort me? What would build me up? What would help me overcome my circumstances?*

Third, they are healers. They provide solutions while others ponder problems. I'm sure other good people looked at the suffering and illnesses afflicting people in third-world countries and saw these immense problems. How could you possibly build enough hospitals in those remote, impoverished areas to serve all those in need? Don and Deyon Stephens saw past the problem and came up with an ingenious solution: convert cruise ships into floating hospitals and staff them with volunteers who travel to wherever there is need.

Fourth, servant leaders also don't bother with short-term fixes. They sow seeds that will have lasting, long-term, and ever-expanding impact. President Sirleaf established peace in her volatile homeland, and then she set about building schools and attracting foreign investments to create opportunities for future generations.

Planters of good seeds keep building upon what they've done, either by growing it themselves or inspiring others to join and surpass them, just as Robert Shumake did in passing on his work with the homeless to Leon and Jennifer Birdd.

Fifth, servant leaders are bridge builders who put aside narrow self-interests in favor of harnessing the power of many to bring about change for the benefit of all. They believe in abundance, that there are rewards enough for everyone when both goals and successes are shared. Where some leaders believe in divide and conquer, servant leaders believe in building a community of men and women with a common purpose.

I saw the power of this bridge-building trait exemplified most recently while attending an event called I Heart Central Oregon in which more than twenty-five hundred volunteers from three counties and seventy churches from a range of denominations came together to plant good seeds in their communities. The organizer of this event, Jay Smith, brought me in to speak to his volunteers and to schoolchildren in the region during an incredible week of faith in action.

Jay and members of the band Elliot have been organizing these events for several years, and the great thing is that they bring all these people from several denominations together to serve people in the community. They don't just talk the talk; they walk the walk. They go out on Saturdays in a mass volunteer movement and paint fire hydrants, repair homes, rake leaves, mow lawns, run errands, move furniture, and do whatever else they can to make a difference in the lives of their neighbors.

I told Jay that it's really difficult to figure out who the organizers are at these events, because everyone takes a leadership role in whatever way they are willing to serve and care. It's interesting that Jay came up with his multidenominational days of community service at a time in his life when he was hurting. He had been involved in missionary work around the world for fifteen years, traveling to twenty-four nations and working with innumerable young volunteers. Then, in 2006, Jay went through a difficult season and needed to stay closer to home where he could focus on his family, including his four young children. He was in what he called a "broken season," and he realized his days of traveling the world as a missionary were over, at least for a time. He had moved back to his hometown—Bend, Oregon—where he decided to use at home the energy he'd devoted to doing good things in places like Uganda or Ukraine.

In his season of hardship, this servant leader didn't dwell on his own hurt, but instead he reached out to help others. Bend is a relatively affluent resort and retirement town, but many of the outlying towns are struggling because of the economic downturn as well as drugs and violence. So Jay decided to focus his efforts in the needy areas.

"We had no money, but we went ahead and set up our first service project with one hundred fifty volunteers from several different churches— only to have it snow a foot that day," he said. "So our service project plan was snowed out. Instead, we grabbed shovels, trucks, and snowplows and spent the day clearing driveways and sidewalks for people. While doing this, we discovered and helped many elderly people who were shut-ins and others who couldn't get out because of the snow."

They were talking to one elderly man as he tried to shovel snow off his roof. While he was speaking, he fainted from exhaustion. Some of the volunteers took care of him and finished the job. The day of service and collaborative effort ended with a celebration: a concert by Elliot, which is a key element of these events. They drew nearly seven hundred teens. At an altar call that night, more than one hundred twenty received Christ.

The success of that first service event, despite the snowfall, put Jay's and the band's faith into action in a big way. Over the years that followed, they organized fifteen similar I Heart events in eleven Oregon cities, sometimes with as many as twenty-five hundred volunteers from seventy churches doing service work in their communities. I know, because I spoke at several of those events. In 2010 I appeared before more than eight thousand people for an I Heart Central Oregon event at the Expo Center.

We added to that event with a little I Hug fun prior to my speech, setting the world record for the most hugs in sixty minutes. I managed to hug 1,749 people in one hour. You can see the video on YouTube.com. Comedian Nick Cannon, who is married to singer Mariah Carey, tried to break our record, but he couldn't do it. I guess he just wasn't properly armed to take me on!

Jay's more serious goal in these I Heart events is to show the power of Christian faith in action by serving the community while also opening up lines of communication and breaking down walls between churches and church denominations. "Sometimes churches tend to look at all other denominations as different. They don't often interact. But I have many friends across church lines, and I see the value of all denominations," he said. "We can never contain Christ in one church, and together we can show the different facets of faith, whether it's Nazarenes, Baptists, Foursquares, Catholics, Presbyterians, Methodists, and everything in between. I think it's hard for people to listen to Christians if they don't see us living our faith, so our model is love in action."

Like me, Jay believes that our churches hold the hope of the world. While I can come into a place as an evangelist and offer inspiration, motivation, and hope, it is the church and its ministry that is there day in and day out to serve and love the people of their community. That's why it bothers us that too often churches don't work together to multiply their blessings.

"Jesus said, 'By this everyone will know that you are my disciples, if you love one another,' and I feel it is in His heart that we come together," Jay said. "We are better together than we are apart, and churches are realizing that their doctrinal differences are less important. The main thing is that we believe Jesus Christ is the way to salvation. That is our most important similarity. If we are humble enough, we can work past our differences and come together for the good of all."

Along with humility and a focus on the common good, a big part of being a servant leader is listening to what others need rather than imposing on them what you want for them. Jay is sensitive to the fact that some churches have fewer resources than others, so he always tries to keep costs down by getting grants to avoid putting any financial pressure on the participants.

In one Oregon city with many living in poverty, Jay and his team raised more than enough money through grants and donations for their project. In fact, they had seven hundred dollars left over from the event. One of the church pastors involved suggested a novel idea for using that money during the Christmas season: they disbursed the money in five-dollar increments to church members and gave them the mission to grow and multiply that seed money for charitable purposes any way they could, whether it was buying candy at a discount and selling it, using it to make lemonade for a lemonade stand, or buying gas for mowing lawns.

The seven hundred dollars was multiplied into *ten thousand* dollars and used to fund projects like care packages for the homeless, helping single moms buy Christmas presents, providing stuffed animals for abused children, and other creative acts of kindness.

"We do this to show our love through serving others. It's a way of letting communities know that their churches care. We're not preaching down to them, we are serving up to them," Jay said. "And we don't intend for our days of service to be a one-time event. Often, after we've gone, the relationship continues to grow between the churches and cities. We've seen it develop where mayors can call pastors and ask for a congregation to put on their work clothes and lend a hand. Once people have tasted the joy of service, they want to stay involved."

Jay and his army of servant leaders have had some unusual requests when they offer their services. "We tell them we have five hundred volunteers, so what can we do for their city? One town couldn't afford to mow its overgrown cemeteries because of budget cuts, so the churches did it, and now they have taken on that responsibility. It's opened up new ways for churches to serve their communities."

Officials in the city of Bend said they couldn't afford to repaint their fire hydrants, which is necessary every few years so that they can be quickly spotted in an emergency. During three I Heart events over two years, volunteers repainted thirty-six hundred hydrants, saving the city thousands of dollars. The idea is to let each city determine how it can be served, which helps build enthusiasm and goodwill. In some cities Jay and his crew also partner with nonprofits like local food banks, soup kitchens, women's shelters, Head Start, or Habitat for Humanity.

"We just come in as a catalyst. Oftentimes, pastors are hesitant at first, but then the walls come down once we are all praying and eating and working together. It's like the momentum builds, and then the next city we go to has heard about what happened in the previous city, and they are more open to working together."

I'm very happy to say that Jay has recently moved to California, where he and I hope to work together on a series of events in which we do just that: putting love and faith into action to serve others and to lead by our example.

You know the great thing about sowing good seeds as a servant leader is that it really doesn't take big projects like those that Jay is so good at organizing. Even small acts of humble giving can make a huge difference for someone. Jay reminded me of one such thing that occurred at one of his events in Oregon.

I was zipping around the area, trying to hit a bunch of high schools one day. After speaking at one particular school, we were rushing for the door because we were running late (as usual). I didn't have time to offer hugs to anyone in the audience who wanted to come up, which is very unusual for me. (I do like my hug time.)

On the way out of the school auditorium, I happened to glimpse a bald head, which isn't something you normally see in a crowd of teenagers. I stopped my wheelchair and backed up and saw that it was a girl who appeared to have lost her hair to chemotherapy. I visit a lot of cancer patients. I know the look.

I maneuvered my chair close to her seat at the end of an aisle and said,

"Sweetheart, give me a hug." Needless to say, I was no longer worried about being late to the next speech. She put her arms around me, and soon she was crying and I was crying and every teacher and student around us was crying.

Why did we cry? I can't tell you for certain what was going on with her or with the others around us, but for me, it was gratitude for the gift of serving someone in need. It is difficult for me to capture in words, but this e-mail sent to me by a young girl I'll call Bailey sums up the life-changing experience of servant leadership much better than I can.

Twelve years ago, my mother dragged me out to volunteer at a camp for adults with developmental disabilities. At this Christian camp, each volunteer would be paired one on one with an adult with a disability for an entire week. For twelve-year-old me, there was nothing else that could possibly have been worse than being forced to spend a week with people with disabilities.

My mom didn't give me an option, and she sure didn't give me a way out of this "terrible" situation. My stomach was in knots as I sat nervously throughout orientation. Later on in the day, the camp staff handed out the applications for our campers and under the "disability" section, there it was, written in big, bold, fear-inducing letters: Down syndrome.

My hands shook as I flipped through the application that had just been given to me as I tried to prepare myself for meeting my camper the next day. I tossed and turned all night, questioning why God would put me in a situation where I was so fearful and so uncomfortable.

After breakfast and more orientation the next morning, the

campers began to arrive, which made me more terrified than I could imagine. I could identify each of the campers that stepped out of the cars, but it was not by name that I was identifying them—it was by their disability—Down syndrome, autism, cerebral palsy. It was truly all I could see as the campers continued to arrive.

Finally, my name was called as a small girl quietly slid out of the van at the welcome area. I sheepishly walked over as the camp director introduced me to my camper for the week, Schanna. I didn't know what to say other than "hello," but before I could get that simple word out, Schanna had already thrown her arms around my neck and had begun to embrace me with an all-encompassing hug that I had never felt before.

"I can't wait to be best friends with you this week," she said, grabbing my hand and pulling me off to the first camp activity.

How could someone who just met me love me so unconditionally? They didn't know my grades in school or how many friends I had or how popular I was. They didn't know any of the things that previously defined me as a human being. By that evening every wall of insecurity, every hedge of fear had been completely and entirely broken down by an adult with a developmental disability, and all it took was giving Schanna a chance to be my friend.

It's been twelve years since my first week of camp. After that week, my mom no longer had to drag me kicking and screaming out to other weeks of it. On my own accord I attended over thirty more weeks of camp across those twelve years, not only returning as a volunteer, but later as a summer intern.

The past two summers, I've even been on staff as an assistant camp director, and nothing gives me more joy than seeing first-time volunteers come out to a week of camp, knees trembling, hearts aching, and seeing their walls get shattered by a population that our society completely overlooks.

God has blessed me beyond measure throughout my time at camp. He has instilled in me a love and a passion for the population that our camp serves, and I am certain that anyone who gives someone with a disability a chance will have their life changed in absolutely incredible ways. Not only have our campers taught me how to pray and talk to God openly, but they have also taught me how to love unconditionally and to freely share my faith with others.

In the ninth chapter of John, Jesus is asked, "Who sinned, this man or his parents, that he was born blind?" and Jesus answers, "Neither this man nor his parents sinned; but this happened so that God's works might be revealed in him."

I am so thankful that our Father in heaven has allowed people to be born with what our society calls "disabilities." It is those people who have the power to positively impact our world and ultimately influence others for Christ. They, to me, are not the disabled. The disabled are people like me who look down on others, who doubt God's plan for my life, who are afraid to talk about God to others, and who have a hard time being vulnerable to the people around me. It is the population that our society and even our churches so often overlook that took my hand and led me into God's promises and who have changed my life countless times in unimaginable ways.

Because of my time at camp and the countless hours I've spent serving alongside adults with developmental disabilities, I will be attending graduate school in the fall to attain a degree in counseling with a career goal of one day providing counseling services for parents who find out their kids have disabilities—whether it's when parents find out their child will have an extra chromosome before they're even born or when a parent starts to notice later on that their child is presenting the signs of autism.

It is my passion and dream to help empower our society to not only accept people with disabilities but also to minister *with* people with disabilities to help influence people for Christ, one person at a time!

Bailey expresses the joys of servant leadership beautifully in her e-mail, don't you think? When you serve others, your own heart heals. One of the greatest joys I've received is the joy of watching someone else succeed or serving as a lifeline to encourage and inspire another person. Bailey balked at first, but she learned a wonderful lesson while working in that camp. I think it's a great experience when younger people participate in servant leadership as she did—whether it's volunteering in a nursing home, working with the disabled, or helping in a shelter.

I encourage you to sow good seeds by serving others. You may find, as Bailey did, that the life you transform is your own.

TEN

Living in Balance

I TRIED TO BRING A SMILE TO THE REVEREND BILLY GRAHAM AT OUR first meeting, but at the age of ninety-two, the famed evangelist had more serious business. He wanted to speak to my heart and soul.

Kanae and I were invited to meet Reverend Graham at his North Carolina mountain home by his evangelist daughter, Anne Graham Lotz, whom I met at a conference in Switzerland in 2011. We were thrilled to receive the invitation, and a month later we made the trip. Our excitement was heightened by the beauty of the drive to the family's cabin. It was surreal. As we climbed higher and higher into the Blue Ridge Mountains, the blue sky grew more vibrant and vivid with each turn in the road. Heaven seemed within reach.

Maybe it was the elevation and the thin air, but I also began to feel a little anxious, which is unusual for me. The thought of meeting Reverend

Graham, my evangelistic role model, was daunting, given his accomplishments and place in history. He has traveled to one hundred eighty-seven nations, served as the spiritual advisor to world leaders, preached to billions of people in person and on television, and led more than three million individuals to accept Jesus Christ as their personal Savior. In the last five years, the Billy Graham Evangelistic Association launched a worldwide television program, and through that venture alone, an additional seven million souls have been added to those numbers.

At his last public appearance, the minister known as America's Pastor spoke to more than 230,000 people. It was planned to be the last of his 418 crusades and was held in 2005 for three days in New York City. In his lifetime, Reverend Graham reached out to the world through many platforms. I especially admired how he called upon Christian churches of all denominations to work together in serving God and His children.

Recently, health problems have limited his public appearances, but Reverend Graham still looms large as an international figure. Someone reminded me that President Obama had driven up this same mountain road to see him just a few months before us. That didn't help to calm me.

When Reverend Graham welcomed us to his home, I tried to break the ice with a little joke. He did not crack a smile. In fact, he ignored my nervous attempt at humor.

"When Anne told me that you were coming, I was very excited because I've been hearing about your ministry," he said. "The Lord woke me at three this morning to pray for our meeting."

Anne, who was with us that day, had warned that her father had been ill with pneumonia and other afflictions. She said he might tire easily, and although he appeared frail, when he spoke to us, his voice was strong and very familiar to someone who had so often heard him speak.

Reverend Graham let me know that he saw me as one of the next generation, an heir to his evangelistic mission, and he wanted to prepare me with words of wisdom and encouragement. He said we lived in exciting times, and no matter what adversity we had to go through as evangelists, our job was to preach the gospel of Jesus Christ.

I told him about my travels around the world and even to Muslim countries. He cautioned me not to preach against other religions and not to tell followers of any other religion they were wrong, but instead to "always go in love and respect" and that my only agenda should be to share the gospel.

"Your job is to preach the truth and only the truth of the gospel without targeting certain people or groups," Reverend Graham said. "The truth is powerful, and it will set hearts free."

Reverend Graham congratulated Kanae and me on our marriage plans and told us to marry quickly. Then he prayed for our ministry and us. It was a wonderful meeting. Talking to him was like speaking to an Old Testament figure, such as Abraham or Moses, because he has been such a key person in our spiritual lives for so long.

Reverend Graham touched us deeply in his humanity. He humbly reflected on his life while nibbling on chocolate chip cookies. He told us that he misses his wife, Ruth, who passed away in 2007. He said his only regrets were that he hadn't memorized more Scripture, and in a testament to his faith, Reverend Graham said that he should have spent more time at the feet of Jesus, telling Him how much he loves Him!

I'm sure Reverend Graham has forgotten more Scripture than the rest of us will ever know, and I'm equally certain that he expresses his love for our Lord far more than most. Yet this legendary evangelist, who has also talked about wishing he'd spent more time with his family, wishes he had done even more to show his faith and love of God.

These reflections from one of my major role models inspired me to make adjustments to my ministry now that I am no longer a lone wolf. I already find it difficult to be away from Kanae for more than a day or two. She and I hope to have at least four children, and I want to be there as they grow up.

I also would like to be around a long time for my family, so my plan is to cut back on my traveling. I will be reaching out with my message more through larger venues and larger events, with groups of churches working together and through the media and social networks. Already we have launched a radio program for all ages, and I hope one day to broadcast over the Internet too.

A BALANCED PLAN FOR LIFE

Listening to Reverend Graham reflect on his long and illustrious career as an evangelist caused me to step back and think about what I want to look back on when I reach a similar place in my life. We can easily get caught up in the day-to-day challenges of making a living, overcoming obstacles, dealing with circumstances, and basically surviving that we may neglect relationships, spiritual growth, a deeper understanding of the world, and even our long-term health.

You and I should not live with the expectations that happiness will come *some* day after we accomplish *some* goal or acquire *some* thing. Happiness should be available to you in each moment, and the way to access it is to live in balance spiritually, mentally, emotionally, and physically.

One way to determine the balance that works for you is to look toward the end of your life and then live so that you will have no regrets when you arrive there. The idea is to create a clear image of the type of person you want to be as you age and the mark you hope to make, so that every step of your journey takes you closer to where you want to arrive.

I believe if you create the life you want in your imagination, it is possible to create it in reality minute by minute, hour by hour, and day by day. Instead of a business plan or a house plan, consider this your life plan. Some advise that the way to do this is to think about your own funeral and ponder what you would want your family and friends to say about you, your character, your accomplishments, and how you impacted their lives. Maybe that works for you, but I don't like to think about leaving my loved ones behind—even if I'm going to be with God in heaven.

Instead, I prefer to put myself in Reverend Graham's position on that day we met in his mountain cabin. Here was this great man nearing the end of a remarkable life in which he'd done so much of God's work, and he still had a few regrets. It may be inevitable. Few achieve a perfectly balanced life, but I think it's worth a try. I hope you do too.

I don't want to have any regrets at all, which may not be possible. But I'm going to do my best. So I've reset the Nick lifemeter with the needle on Balance. You might take a moment to do the same if you feel, as I do, that we all need to pause now and then to examine where we've been, where we are now, where we want to go, and how to become a person who will be remembered for making a positive difference in the world.

Even without the benefit of legs, I've spent most of my twenties running at full speed, which is probably what you'd expect of a young single guy with a global ministry and a business too. I've tended to carry the weight of the world on my shoulders. With my nonprofit and my business, I've borne a lot of responsibility. Reverend Graham advised me to share more of the burden and to enjoy a more balanced life built around my faith and my family. I think God must have been talking through His faithful

servant Billy Graham, because I'd also heard that message at the Switzerland conference where I met his daughter.

Taking the Global View

Anne Graham Lotz and I both attended the World Economic Forum
(WEF) in Davos in 2011. I was on a panel for the last event of the forum,
a session titled "Inspired for a Lifetime." My fellow panelists were inspiring
beyond words. They included the German economist Klaus Schwab, who
is founder and chairman of the World Economic Forum, and Christine
Lagarde, who was then France's minister of economic affairs, finances,
and industry but shortly thereafter was named to lead the International
Monetary Fund. Also on the panel were two young dynamos from the
Global Changemakers organization—a global community of young activists, innovators, and entrepreneurs—Daniel Joshua Cullum of New Zea-
land and Raquel Helen Silva of Brazil.

As others have noted, the World Economic Forum is sometimes characterized unfairly as a very dry meeting in which "gray men in gray suits
with gray imaginations get together to schmooze." In truth, it is a meeting
of more than two thousand diverse men and women, most of them leaders
in their fields, and the topics cover a wide and fascinating range. Our session was far from dry. In fact, everyone on the panel and in the packed
audience had tears in their eyes at one point or another.

Remarkably, I received at least two hugs from Christine Lagarde that
day! She was very warm to me and said I inspired her with my work. I'm
sure my former professors of financial planning and accounting would
have been proud to see their student so kindly treated by the soon-to-be
head of the International Monetary Fund. (You can see my presentation on

YouTube.com just by searching for my name and "World Economic Forum." The video of our session is one of the most viewed on the Internet from the 2011 forum.)

Our discussion in Switzerland focused on finding ways to make the world a better place, and we delved into spiritual matters as well. Anne Graham Lotz recalled that the entire forum had a very spiritual element to it, which is unusual. Professor Schwab himself said during the event that answers to the problems the world is facing politically and economically will come from the faith community, in which he included Christians, Muslims, Hindus, and Buddhists.

Anne Graham Lotz later wrote on her website (www.annegraham lotz.com) that at the forum she "saw Jesus in righteousness and justice, shaking the world's business and economic leaders by exposing the greed and self-serving interests that have dominated policies for decades. As a result, many leaders now seem open to the need for shared values, and are looking for answers beyond the traditional bastions of power and conventional wisdom. Could God be allowing the world to face problems that seem to have no human solution, so that its leaders will look up? God will give them wisdom, insight, and solutions that are beyond their considerable intellectual knowledge and experience if they will turn to Him."

Like Anne, I was heartened by the open discussions on the power of faith in action at this gathering of global leaders. Of course, it didn't escape me that I was a guest speaker at the World Economic Forum just shortly after experiencing my own personal economic crisis. God really does have a sense of humor, doesn't He?

As I mentioned earlier, I also believe God was trying to deliver a message about leading a more balanced life at the forum, as well as through Reverend Graham at his cabin a few months later. In fact, the message in

Davos came from the WEF founder himself. Our panel leader, Professor Schwab, spoke about managing a personal balance sheet, which, unlike a business balance sheet, should show that at the end of your life, you gave out more than you took in. Christine Lagarde, who knows a thing or two about balance sheets, added that even when our lives aren't in perfect balance, we can make contributions to the lives of others, even if all we have to give is a smile or a kind word.

FULL ENGAGEMENT

When such wise people talk of living in balance, we should feel encouraged to find fulfillment in all aspects of life—in mind, body, heart, and spirit—so that you keep growing and thriving in your mental prowess, your physical health, your emotional well-being, and in the strength of your faith.

Maintaining an absolutely perfect balance in all four areas is probably not a realistic goal with all the pressures in our lives. After all, our poor brains can get overtaxed, our bodies break down, relationships ebb and flow, and living according to our faith requires constant vigilance and adjustments. Still, being aware of each element and striving to achieve balance is a worthy goal. My hope is that I'll be able to reach the end of my life and know that I've done my best, as imperfect as I may be.

With Kanae in my life now, and with our plans to begin a family someday, I want to take care of myself for the sake of those I love. I can no longer selfishly stress my body by working too hard, not eating well, and neglecting to exercise. I have to remain in control of my emotions so that I can put my wife first by being attentive, encouraging, and supportive of her needs in that arena. Mentally, I want to keep growing my knowledge base so that I can keep up with her and be a source of wisdom for our children. Spiritually, well, this is an especially critical area for both of us since we hope to work together as Christian evangelists who inspire and lead others to Jesus Christ, our Lord and Savior.

We all have to decide what works best for us, fulfills us, and gives us the greatest sense of control and contentment in our interior and exterior lives. If you are feeling out of sync, stuck, unmotivated, or unloved, then you may need to get back into alignment. Reflect on each area of your life and consider whether you've paid enough attention to each. Then devise a plan for addressing anything you've neglected in the physical, emotional, mental, and spiritual realms.

A few things to keep in mind when seeking balance:

1. You are uniquely made, so you must determine what "balance" means for you based on your circumstances, relationships, and needs. A single person will surely have different criteria than someone who is married or a parent. As your situation and circumstances change, your balance will likely shift. The important thing is to be aware of the need to maintain harmony in all areas of your life and to stand ready to make adjustments when needed.

2. Maintaining balance is not about being in control. You can't control all aspects of life anymore than you can control every driver and every car on the road with you. The best you can do is to remain alert to all possibilities and be flexible and thoughtful in your responses.

3. Don't feel you have to go it alone. Australians and Americans especially suffer from the solitary hero or Lone Ranger complex. My parents will enjoy this one because their son Nick wasn't the best at sharing his feelings and listening to advice in his younger years. Often, I had to do things my way, and that led to many lessons learned the hardheaded way. You will probably make the same mistakes, but at least be open to the possibility that those

who care the most about you may have some advice worth heeding. Consider that maybe they aren't trying to control you. Instead, they may be trying to help you. Listening to them is not a sign of weakness or dependence. It is a sign of strength and maturity.

4. Go with your gifts and passions. The most balanced, stable, happy, and fulfilled people I know are those who build their lives around the continuous development and full expression of their talents and interests. They don't have jobs or even careers. They have passion and purpose. They are fully engaged. If you do what you love and earn a living from it, you will never have to work a day in your life, and retirement will be what other people do.

5. When you aren't getting what you want, try giving it. If you can't catch a break, why not provide one? If no one is reaching out to you, reach out to someone whose needs are greater than yours. Take the focus off your problems and help someone deal with theirs. What have you got to lose other than self-pity? Sometimes the best way to heal your own body, mind, heart, and spirit is to serve as a source of comfort and support to someone around you. Filling the bucket of someone else may replenish your own.

6. Live in a constant state of gratitude, and laugh whenever possible. You will have days in which life seems to drop one load of bricks after another on you. The best way to escape that pile is to rise above it. Gratitude and good humor are the great elevators of life. Instead of cursing the bricks that bruise you, be thankful for the opportunity to face challenges and grow from them. If nothing else, simply give thanks to God for another day and the chance to make a difference, to take another step forward, to laugh with those you love.

FOR EVERYTHING THERE IS A SEASON

We are all connected. We all have the same basic human needs to love and be loved. We all want to serve a purpose and to know that our lives have value. Living in balance also means living in harmony with others, which may require giving up yourself to share in something greater—a fuller life.

I was a single man for so long that when I finally found a loving relationship, I had to make some quick adjustments. I had wanted to share my life with someone, but in some ways I wasn't prepared for what that actually meant. My balance was thrown off because my life was no longer just mine. It was like having someone else jump into your canoe. Suddenly, everything shifts. You have to adjust your position. The load is greater but so is your paddle power. Now, it is a matter of working together to get where you both want to go while keeping the boat upright.

Suddenly Kanae's wants, needs, and feelings are a consideration. What is important to her has to become important to me. All our relationships are intertwined. Now, my priorities are God, Kanae, our family and friends, and everything else, in that order.

My goal, which I hope you will share with me, is to always put my unstoppable faith into action so that the love of God in my heart is obvious in the way I treat and serve my wife and everyone else in my life. To have faith is not enough. You have to exercise your faith, act upon it, and share it so that others are inspired to love God as you do.

Some people know the Word of God and go to church, but they don't know the power of the Holy Spirit. They don't have a personal relationship with the Lord, which comes only when you step out and put your faith into action. I've learned that whenever I live to honor God and serve others, He multiplies the blessings.

I have been tremendously blessed to have such a wonderful board of directors and staff at Life Without Limbs. They encourage me, pray for me, and are used by God to keep me grounded. I have my uncle Batta Vujicic, who was instrumental in believing that the Lord did indeed call me to be a vessel for His use. He saw this ten years ago and was used by the Lord to help establish a base and headquarters in the United States, together with the other board members: David Price, Don McMaster, and Reverend Dan'l Markham. I am blessed to have people who believe in the ministry of Life Without Limbs. They not only pray for us but also financially support us to help us serve and inspire millions of people around the world.

Many people support me with their prayers, which have been a great source of strength and encouragement. Uncle Batta had a vision that encouraged me, and this is his description of it:

> Several years ago, Nick came to our home to join our family circle for dinner and to relax. After dinner we spent a substantial part of the evening strategizing and planning new ministry visions and activities. It was that night after Nick went home that I had a dream that was very real and vivid.
>
> When I woke up, I shared my experience with my wife, Rita. In my vision I was in a large assembly when an unidentified person got up and with a loud voice aggressively asked me, "Who is Nick Vujicic?" Without further thoughts my instant reply to that person was, "Look up Acts 9:15."
>
> That scenario repeated itself, but it was another person from the same assembly who asked me the same question in a loud and insistent voice, "Who is Nick Vujicic?"

I repeated my answer, "Look up Acts 9:15."

After verbalizing my dream to my wife, I asked her if she knew what this passage in Acts 9:15 was saying. Neither one of us at the time knew what the verse contained, so we reached for the Bible, opened up to the book of Acts 9:15. This is what that scripture says, "Go thy way: for he is a chosen vessel unto me, to bear my name before the Gentiles, and kings, and the children of Israel."

That following Sunday, I shared my vision with our congregation of the La Puente Church as a testimony for Nick's ministry and his involvement in furthering the gospel of Jesus Christ and His kingdom. I have declared my testimony of this vision and will continue to do so with a firm belief that Nick is a chosen vessel of the Lord. It is evident that Nick's fulfillment of the Great Commission is in the heart of the Life Without Limbs ministry and is aligned with our Lord's commandment as stated in Mark 16:15, "Go ye into all the world, and preach the gospel to every creature."

Further, a similar parallel account is declared in Revelation 14:6–7: "And I saw another angel fly in the midst of heaven, having the everlasting gospel to preach unto them that dwell on the earth, and to every nation, and kindred, and tongue, and people, saying with a loud voice, Fear God, and give glory to him; for the hour of his judgment is come: and worship him that made heaven, and earth, and the sea, and the fountains of waters." Also in Mark 13:10: "And the gospel must first be published among all nations."

The vision that I had years ago and the overwhelming evidence of the Lord's opening countless doors for the ministry in order for Nick to declare the Good News continues to be an encouragement to me. As the Lord guides me, I will continue supporting Nick and the ministry of Life Without Limbs, both as a brother and director of that nonprofit organization, as long as I am confident that he has not compromised doctrinal truths and that he has not jeopardized the position of being a chosen vessel of God—and as long as he remains faithful, transparent, sincere, humble, and meek.

As you can tell, Uncle Batta helps keep me focused on my purpose, and he makes sure that I put my faith into action. As I walk through doors of opportunity to share the love and hope I have found, my life keeps on getting richer and more joyful and fulfilled. Whether I speak at schools, corporations, seminars, conferences, the congresses of nations, or to orphans, former sex slaves, or presidents, I am always asked, "But how did you do it? How did you get through your depression, and what is the foundation of hope you have found?"

My life is built upon my faith and the teachings of the Scriptures. These are the source of my confidence, my belief system, my decisiveness, my persistence, and my endurance. With faith guiding my deeds, I can find balance in mind, body, heart, and spirit.

Whenever I need inspiration to act upon my faith, I think of my Serbian grandparents who were persecuted for their Christian beliefs. The communist government did not allow them to worship freely. To live their faith, they had to flee their homeland, which is how I came to grow up in Australia. Both of my grandfathers are in heaven now, I'm sure, but I did have the opportunity to seek their advice while they were here.

My dad's father always told me to "believe and be disciplined" in my faith. He referred to Psalm 1:3, which says, "He shall be like a tree planted by the rivers of water, that brings forth its fruits in its season, whose leaf also shall not wither; and whatever he does shall prosper." When you are deeply rooted in faith, you are unstoppable.

My mum's father encouraged me in much the same way that Reverend Graham did. He said, "Preach the gospel, don't add or subtract from it." He, too, believed that God's truth sets us free.

I am blessed to have come from such a wise and spiritual family. With their continuing support, I want to be unstoppable in inspiring people by telling them about the love and hope I've found in my faith and the wonderful results I've seen from putting it in action. I hope you have drawn strength and inspiration from this book. Jesus provides my strength. He uses me for His purpose. My calling is to encourage others to find their own purpose and fulfillment and, if possible, to help them find a path to happiness everlasting. I know that God loves the world. He loves you so much He made sure you read this book so you could be encouraged by it! I love you and I pray for you. Thank you for your love and prayers in return.

ACKNOWLEDGMENTS

MOST OF ALL, I THANK GOD: FATHER, SON, AND HOLY SPIRIT.

Words cannot express my joy in being able to thank my wife, Kanae, for all the love, care, support, and prayers she gives in abundance to me. I love you, *mi amor*!

I'd like to thank my parents, Boris and Dushka Vujicic, for being such strong pillars of support throughout my life. Thanks, Mum and Dad. My brother, Aaron, the best man at my wedding—thank you and your wife, Michelle, for loving me and keeping me grounded. Michelle, my sister— thanks for believing in me and my dreams. To the new family I now have, the Miyahara and Osuna families, my mother-in-law, Esmeralda, my new brothers Keisuke, Kenzi, and Abraham, and my new sister Yoshie—thank you for loving and accepting me into your family.

Thanks again to my relatives and friends who throughout the years have supported me and sown encouragement each step of the way—you all played a part, and I thank you. George Miksa—I pray the Lord continues to carry you and lead you and bless you for helping me start the headquarters of Life Without Limbs in the United States.

Thank you to the board of directors of Life Without Limbs and their families: Batta Vujicic, David Price, Dan'l Markham, Don McMaster, Terry Moore, and Jon Phelps. Thank you, as well, to the advisory board of Life Without Limbs. A very big thank-you to the faithful, diligent, and faith-filled staff of Life Without Limbs. Keep up the great work. Thank you to Ignatius Ho, who helps direct our Hong Kong Life Without Limbs chapter. Thank you to the Apostolic Christian Church of the Nazarene, especially Pasadena, for your support. Thank you also to the Attitude Is Altitude staff and team for backing me, praying for me, and believing with me.

I would like to say a very special thank-you to Wes Smith and his wife, Sarah, for their support. Wes, I could not have asked for a better writing partner. I am very proud of the two books we've written so far.

Thanks once again to my literary agents, Jan Miller Rich and Nena Madonia at Dupree Miller & Associates, who have had faith in me and my purpose from the beginning. Also my deepest thanks to my publisher, WaterBrook Multnomah, a division of Random House, and its sterling team, including Michael Palgon, Gary Jansen, Steve Cobb, and Bruce Nygren, who have encouraged and supported me.

Last, but not less important, thank you to all the people who pray for me, my wife, our ministry, and to those who financially support us. A big thank-you as well for helping us attain the goals of Life Without Limbs.

Bless all who read this book. I pray that my words open your hearts and minds in a fresh and dynamic way, moving you to put your faith into action while inspiring others to do the same.

ABOUT THE AUTHOR

NICK VUJICIC is a motivational speaker, evangelist, author, and the director of the nonprofit organization Life Without Limbs. Nick has become a great inspiration to people around the world, regularly speaking to large crowds about overcoming obstacles and achieving dreams.

A longtime resident of Australia, he now lives in Southern California with his wife, Kanae. Visit his websites at www.LifeWithoutLimbs.org and www.AttitudeIsAltitude.com.

YOU CAN MAKE A DIFFERENCE

HOPE revives a desperate soul.
HOPE inspires and heals.

It changes a life, and that one life can change the world.
Nick found true hope in the saving grace of Jesus.

Your gifts, both large and small, will allow us to reach
more people around the world with this life-changing hope!

DONATE TODAY!

LIFE WITHOUT LIMBS

VISIT US
LIFEWITHOUTLIMBS.ORG

WRITE US
P.O. BOX 2430
AGOURA HILLS, CA 91376

CONTACT US
TOLL FREE
855-303-LIFE (5433)